# People are talking about
## *The Recipe…*

"The Recipe *is a gem of a book. It offers important and easily actionable lessons on leadership and team-building for both your professional and personal life---and it does so in the most delightful, whimsical way."*
--- **Monica Crowley**, Panelist, "The McLaughlin Group," News Analyst, Fox News Channel, and Nationally Syndicated Radio Host. www.MonicaMemo.com

"The Recipe *is a great guide for business leaders especially those in rapidly growing companies."*
--- **Todd Davis**, CEO, LifeLock  www.lifelock.com

" *Want the recipe for entrepreneurial success? Step one: be a sharp leader. Step two: be an artful team-builder. Step three: read* The Recipe. *This book is the perfect resource for both new and seasoned entrepreneurs."*
--- **Mike Michalowicz**, Author of The Toilet Paper Entrepreneur  www.ToiletPaperEntrepreneur.com

"A secret to your success is making the most of family, leadership and teamwork. The Recipe *has the ingredients of all three."*
--- **John Assaraf,** New York Times Bestselling Author, *The Answer* and *Having It All*. www.johnassaraf.com

*"The Recipe contains all the right ingredients for modern, innovative entrepreneurs. The storybook tableau – a sort of Hans Christian Anderson meets Charles Handy – offers uplifting insight on how to collaborate, team build and prosper in our highly networked business world. Whether you're a butcher, a baker or a software maker, you'll enjoy The Recipe."*
--- **Mike Drummond**, editor-in-chief *Inventors Digest* magazine

*"One of my favorite books on business and leadership is the 1921 tale called "The Go Getter," by Peter Bernard Kyne. Amilya's book reminds me why I loved that story so much, and helped inspire me to reinvigorate my entrepreneurial mojo. Yet another reason why I don't hesitate to book Amilya as a guest on any number of business subjects, no matter the new cycle."*
--- **Mike Straka,** Executive Producer, *The Strategy Room*
www.FoxNews/StrategyRoom

*"A wonderful story that shares how to bring individuals together, unifying teams and crystallizing their focus. I highly recommend The Recipe."*
--- **Chip Conley**, Founder and CEO, Joie de Vivre Hospitality & Author, *PEAK: How Great Companies Get Their Mojo from Maslow.*

# THE
# RECIPE

## BY AMILYA ANTONETTI

# The Recipe
## By Amilya Antonetti

Compete ordering information for individual and quantity sales is
available at www.Amilya.com/TheRecipe/Orders

**⊙ Core**Purpose™

CorePurpose Publishing
Joan Koerber-Walker, Publisher and Managing Editor
PO Box 51060, Phoenix, Arizona 85076-1060
480-921-3933

**The story contained in *The Recipe* is a work of fiction. All
characters are fictional and have no relation to individuals
living or dead.**

ISBN:  978-0-9747056-9-9

Managing Editor, Joan Koerber-Walker
Associate Editor, Terri Elders   Layout by CorePurpose Publishing
Dust Jacket, Cover Design, and Illustrations by Paul Svancara

*This book is dedicated to _you_,*
*the people who are changing the game, building businesses,*
*raising families, and making a difference every day.*

*When we touch a person, it affects a family.*
*When we affect a family, we build a community*
*and together we change the world.*

*Together, all things are possible.*

# Reader's Guide

The wonderful thing about a book like *The Recipe* is that you can experience it for enjoyment or you can use it as a tool to expand your horizons and those of your team, whether your team is at home, at school or in the workplace.

Within the book you have the story of the Givvantake brothers and the team at *Prosperous Bakery*, but you also have Little Spoonfuls of learning aids that accompany many of the sections.

Some readers will enjoy reading the story beginning to end, while others may choose to visit the Little Spoonfuls Appendix as they move from section to section. And that's OK. One of the lessons we've learned along the way is that people learn differently, so this book has been designed so that you can read it in the way that works best for you. You can immerse yourself in the story or do the exercises as they appear. But, either way, Enjoy!

# Table of Contents

# Foreword

If you have not had a chance to meet Amilya Antonetti, here is your opportunity!

If you already know Amilya, you'll recognize her high energy, caring insights, and ebullient straight-talking approach. From the moment you walk into Prosperous Bakery, you'll find she isn't about to waste time setting a complex scene or building an intricate scenario. She is who she is – and meets you on her own terms.

This is a forthright person who calls it as she sees it. The setting she chooses here feels familiar and comfortable. Who doesn't like food, especially that from a fairytale Grandmother and Grandfather? She makes it go down easily.

Yet, Amilya makes it clear, as if there is music in the background that's playing light tunes in a minor key, that she is serving up a simple story that won't be hard to swallow, but will require that we chew on the thoughts she dishes up.

It's not that we do not know where Amilya is going with her story – we've been there. That's why we can settle in, nod in recognition and think about the characters on our teams that fit her description. Yes, they are true to the natural patterns we find in human instincts, and yes, they differ among siblings. And yes, they are the essence of who we are.

When a writer communicates from her instinctive strengths, as happens here, there is a sense of trust that builds with her audience. There is no doubt the *myths* she lists have been thrust at her somewhere, somehow, and she wants to protect us from falling for them.

This is the *Decade of Collaboration*, a time when we must set aside anything akin to sibling rivalries. Our achievements will be because we figured out how to work well with each other, not because we beat others out. By addressing these very issues, this book sets a civil tone that needs to be championed, in a voice that will be heard.

Humility is not the long suit of America's high achievers. What I call *Arrogant Attitude Disorder* has been rampant. The difference between a star and a leader has been cloudy.

Congratulations to Amilya for cutting through all that. Her book provides welcome nutrients for those who desire realistic alliances and shared celebrations. If we incorporate her recipes into our diet they just might make the difference we crave.

Uncluttered with succession plans, performance reviews, turnover rates, job titles and office politics, *The Recipe* helps us focus on basic truths:

- Teams need conflict to have synergy.
- Differences help stir the pot.

- You are who you are, but you can learn tricks to help you self manage your natural abilities.

- Humor and respect are essential ingredients.

Amilya does not lecture about these important recipes for success.

She lets you savor them.


---Kathy Kolbe

Chairman of the Board

Kolbe Corp

Best Selling Author of

- *Pure Instinct: The M.O. of High Performance People and Teams*

- *Powered by Instinct: 5 Rules for Trusting Your Gut* and

- *Conative Connection.*

www.Kolbe.com

# Introduction

Why create <u>another</u> book on leadership and teams?  Why read it?

You would think that with all the great works out there, it would be enough.

Yet all of us struggle in life and in business to find just the right mix of people, with the right talents, and the right attitude, to help us along the journey so that we are not just reacting to life but becoming the leaders in our life, so that we can live a life by design.

In my own journey, I learned a key lesson.  As a leader, I am NOTHING without my team.  It does not matter whether it is in my role as an entrepreneur building successful brands, as a mentor to others who dream of taking their ideas from mind to market, as a friend, or as Mom.  Everything I do I approach with a TEAM mentality.

We each bring unique talents and we need each other if we are to succeed.  Learning HOW to come together in teams can be the secret ingredient that makes the difference in reaching your goals, and that supports you in creating something great, and in living your best life.

Over the past 15 years, I have had the opportunity to share the stories of my journey with live audiences, on television, and on the radio. And what I found was that just as I love to learn through a good story, so do they.

Give me a rhyme, jingle, or story that that I can connect with and I remember it. Show me how something works and I can apply it. Give me the right tools to work with, and I can master them. And, please don't forget the helpful hints and directions. The best lessons are the ones we can quickly learn, grasp the concepts and implement them for our desired results.

So today, when the need for leaders and teams is more important than ever, *The Recipe* is just that. It is a story filled with the kind of characters that we have all met at one time or another along our journeys.

They have a job to do, some things to discover, and some lessons to learn. And, as we join them, we just might learn something too.

Learning how to be *the leader in your own life* and mastering the art of teambuilding is a key life skill. It touches everything we do across our community, our businesses, and our families. My hope is that after reading this book you will never approach any project the same way again, whether you are running your home, your business, or just trying to have more in your life with less resources.

It takes a TEAM to win. And not just any team. You need the right mix of unique ingredients, the right tools, and some easy to follow directions and guidelines. Teams need to know when they are working within them or have stepped out of bounds.

Developing your natural leadership style and learning to building high performance teams does not happen in an instant. It takes time and practice. Not to mention a bit of trial and error. We can't master what we don't practice.

So along with the story, our team has sprinkled *The Recipe* with some "Little Spoonfuls" of ideas, tools, and exercises that you can use along your journey. You will learn more about this in the Reader's Guide.

So enjoy *The Recipe* and getting to know the team at Prosperous Bakery. And always remember,

Together all things ARE possible – it just needs the right TEAM behind it.

Sending Smiles,

*Amilya*

P.S. You can find more information on Amilya.com/TheRecipeInteractive about the *The Recipe* Interactive Teambuilding Sessions. There are also some fabulous tools you can use to help yourself and your team along the journey, and, of course, a place where you can send me a note if you have a story to share.

I hope you will. We want to hear from you!

Please share your *Recipe* stories with me and our team at Amilya.com where we can continue the journey together.

# Acknowledgments

You may see me, but I am NOTHING without my team. *The Recipe* is a great example of that. Our team worked tirelessly to bring together a project that we all are very proud of, not just because it is a great story, but because we created it together by combining our unique talents, and together we shine better than we do apart. There is never an "I". It's always a "WE".

What you hold in your hands is the result of teamwork among a circle of friends, teammates and all of you who have continued to support me as my journey continues to unfold. THANK YOU!

Each member of the team shared a little piece of themselves inside these pages and their contributions live on in this book. Now we are passing it on, opening the circle to you and your teams. Welcome and ENJOY.

I will be eternally grateful to my **Nannie, Mary Korker**, who taught me my very first life lessons in her kitchen.

**My mother** left this world when I was 17 yet continues to watch from above. Thanks to **my father, Franco** , who came to this country to follow his dream and to give us a better chance in life, and to **my brother, Buddy (Franco, Jr.)** , a Marine, whose life exemplifies how blessed I am to be an Italian-American. They both remain a pillar of strength in my foundation.

What can I say about my amazing children, **David,** my teenage son, who has continued to amaze me with his incredible qualities and heart? Your wings are strong, my son, very strong. I am so proud of you. To **my toddler daughter,** may you too build your wings and have the courage and faith to use them when the time is right.

I am so grateful for **the man who has walked this journey by my side**, day after day and year after year. Anthony, you have been my net, champion, confidant, and my hero! There is no combination of words that can ever express how grateful I am for all that you do, give and sacrifice, everyday, for me and our family.

To my close friend **Katherine Sansone**, whose insight into the characters and the lessons they share has been invaluable. Along with her numerous talents to keep me focused and on point. There are not enough words of gratitude. I am blessed to have you in my life. Feel the love.

To **Ms. Joan Koerber-Walker**, if it were not for her 'quick start" talents blended with a strong knowledge of publishing and business, along with incredible work ethics, you would not be holding this book. Can we all send out a team "Go girl Go"! Thank you so much!

**Oprah**, just saying her name out loud empowers me to use my life to its fullest and to continue to "pay it forward." As a guest on her show, she shared a lesson with me that is a very key ingredient to business success."Always sign your own checks." Oprah has led her life as a shining example of leadership and teamwork. I am grateful for all the doors her life has opened, the pathways she has cleared and knowledge that she continues to share. As humbly as I can, I say, "Thank you!!"

What can I say about the one and only **Kathy Kolbe**, author of the groundbreaking book on team building, *Pure Instinct: the M.O. of High Performance People and Teams*, who so generously has shared her wisdom along the way.

**Anthony Tesoriero**, Co-Founder of Lucky Napkin LLC. It was Anthony who first encouraged me to write this book and to share it with you as a story. And he has never stopped cheering me on along the way. His talent in Marketing/Branding, combined with his ability to connect the dots, has been invaluable to me. Thank you so very much!

To my friend **John Assaraf** who has used his life to help so many. He always "pays it forward" and inspires me to do the same. He has been a wonderful role-model and friend. Thank you!

**Monica Crowley**, of Fox News, has lived an amazing journey. She is so giving, supportive, and willing to share her wisdom and experiences. She has a generosity of spirit seldom found in the world of television. Thank you for raising the bar for me so that I can continue to pay it forward as you do. Thank you

**Donny Deutsch**, thanks for all of the great lessons on business and leadership you shared during our time working together on *The BIG Idea with Donny Deutsch*. You have been an inspiration and friend. Thank you.

**Todd Davis**, CEO of LifeLock, thank you for your support and for being a great example of a terrific leader, I am proud to know you and your amazing wife. Thank you for your continued support as I travel on this journey. I am so grateful.

**Ken Colburn**, CEO of Data Doctors, has been a wonderful friend and "Mr. Johnny on the Spot" for all my crazy last minute call-outs for help. Ken, I adore you and your wife. Thank you.

**Chip Conley** inspired me to write my first book *Why David Hated Tuesdays* after we met at his presentation for the YEO/WPO many years ago. He has continued to be a strong supporter of my passions. He is an amazing business leader that I am honored to call a friend.

**Dahlynn McKowen** is a dear friend. She has taught me so much about writing, networking, and living your passion. Thank you!

**Alexis Levi**, thank you so much, you are awesome! You are a shining example of leadership and team building and use your life in so many ways to inspire so many, including me. Thank you!

**Mike Straka**, thank you for taking a risk on me and inviting me on your show" Strategy Room."  Your knowledge of TV and the industry has taught me so much in such a short time. I am eternally grateful.

**Eric Bolling**, thank you so much for having me on your panel on FoxNews "Strategy Room" Your knowledge and experience expands my mind, keeping me in-tune with the ever changing climate of our politics, government and country. Thank you for your continued support.

**Morris Callaman**, there are no right words to describe how grateful I am for your belief in me, my passion and my business. Your insights always not only teach me but challenge me to grow. Thank you!

**Mike Michalowicz**, my fellow CNBC expert from "The Big Idea," I am so happy our friendship continues to grow. You have been a wonderful champion for me and the AMA team. Good things still to come. Thank you!

Big shout out and thank you to **Maria Bailey**. Thank you for your continued support and being a trusted voice for "Blue Suit" moms everywhere.

 **Mike Drummond** and the team at *Inventors Digest*. Big Thank you! I feel so connected to the inventor community. I am honored that you and your team continue to support my voice. As I continue to learn and grow, I promise to pass on the lessons and message directly to those who need the information.

**To the team at CorePurpose Publishing**, for all their help, support, and commitment in meeting our "impossible" deadlines.

To our wonderful editor, **Terri Elders**, who caught all the little mistakes and made *The Recipe* a better read for you.

To **Perry Dear and the team at Sun Fung Catalogs and Books** who walked us though our crazy production schedules.

**To Paul Svancara**, the talented creative director who created our wonderful cover and original images.

To **Glenn Yeffeth**, Publisher of BenBella Books, who shared his insights with us on how to make *The Recipe* a better read.

To our first readers, **Shannon K. Bullard, Morris Callaman, Pam Falk, Susan Keenehan, Katherine Sansone, John R. Schultz,  Paul Svancara**.

To **Al Schmidt, Lisa Ellis, Tami Klages**, and the incredible team at Metro Studios for creating a home for *The Recipe* at Amilya.com.

To **Ralph Ferraro**, Director of The Italian American Press, you are such a great voice for Italian Americans. Thank you for all of your help and support over the years.

To **Rhonda Sprague** of SpragueDesigns.com and her team for sharing their chalkboard image for our Prosperous Bakery menu boards.

And most of all I want to thank **you!** For by purchasing this book you support not just me but the entire team so we can continue our work to do more, reach more, and build a company where together all things are possible not for just one, but for all.

Thank you for taking your time to experience *The Recipe* with us and more importantly for investing your time in the journey to become a better leader and teammate.

Amilya Antonetti

Amilya Antonetti

# THE
# RECIPE

## BY AMILYA ANTONETTI

# Chapter 1 – The Will

It was not the biggest bakery in town and it was not the smallest. But for years it had prospered as a place where the community gathered to share a bite, pick up something for a special occasion, or simply pass the time with its long-time owners, Mom and Pop Givvantake, as they were affectionately known by everyone in town.

Now they were gone and would be missed.

It was time for *Prosperous Bakery* to pass to a new team of owners, six brothers who had grown up surrounded by the smells of baking bread, warm gooey cookies still fresh from the oven, and the sound of quiet conversations and laughter that often rang out amidst the tables where customers would linger with a special treat from the shining glass bakery shelves.

For the first time in many years, *Prosperous Bakery* was closed.

Yesterday, everyone had said their final good-byes to Mom and Pop Givvantake, who had founded the bakery and run it for over 50 years. Mom had passed away quietly in her sleep one evening. Pop was gone the same way just a few days later. "Mom had been his heart," someone had whispered at the funeral, "and when she left, Pop just followed." After the funeral, the lawyers had explained the details of the will in their formal legal way. With the will had been a stack of envelopes that the lawyer handed to Mary Keeper, the Givvantakes' long-time employee and friend. Mary had been a part of *Prosperous Bakery* for as long as the brothers could remember.

"Don't worry," Mary said, looking at each of the brothers in turn. "I know what these are. There is something special here for each of you. Tomorrow, before the sunrise, we'll meet at *Prosperous Bakery* and I will share some of it with you. And together we can plan how *Prosperous Bakery* will re-open again. I'll meet you in the Community Room in the back."

With that she got up from her chair and gave each of the brothers a gentle hug and the first of their grandparent's final gifts - a key to the front door of *Prosperous Bakery*.

And so here they were, on the very first day. Six brothers gathered in the Community Room with cardboard cups of coffee from the gas station down the street.

No one had thought about coming in early to brew a pot. The sun was not even up yet.

They'd simply brought their own.

They talked to pass the time and to cover the strange silence. *Prosperous Bakery* had never been so quiet before -- and it did not feel the same. Something was missing.

They heard the little bells ring above the shop door. Pop Givvantake had hung the string of bells as a gift for his bride when they had opened *Prosperous Bakery* together half a century before.

"The song of the bells is a gift," Mom would say. Each time she heard them she knew that someone had come to share the most precious of gifts, their time. Mom and Pop had great respect for their customers and employees and the gifts they shared. And in return the customers respected Mom and Pop and retuned over and over again to share their time with the *Prosperous Bakery* team. Over the years, the bells had become one of the bakery's familiar traditions for friends and customers alike. Pop would order similar bells as gifts for close friends and family members as housewarming or wedding gifts. Mom liked to say, "When I hear the bells sing, I know family is here."

Mary came in to join them and with her she carried one of *Prosperous Bakery's* white bakery boxes. Upon seeing her, the brothers became quiet. Mary came forward and set the box at her place at the foot of the big oak table.

Acknowledging each of the young men with a smile and a nod, she walked to the sideboard to take out the white china plates and the silverware sets carefully wrapped in cloth napkins, and set them before each of the brothers.

Then she walked back to her place and opened the bakery box. The scent of vanilla and cinnamon filled the air as she passed the box of handmade cinnamon buns around the table. They were still warm from her oven at home and just like the ones the Givvantakes used to make.

The room was silent as the brothers savored the rolls.

This is more like the *Prosperous Bakery* I remember, each brother thought. The scents and flavors brought back memories of Mom and Pop. They could almost hear Pop's booming voice coming from the kitchen or Mom's quiet laughter from the café.

Then Mary's voice broke the silence of the room as she opened another of the envelopes and read:

> *"To our six wonderful grandsons, we leave equally our most valuable treasure, Prosperous Bakery.*
>
> *We also leave to you The Recipe, which has been the key to Prosperous Bakery's success.*

This recipe has brought us great abundance and happiness. Cherish both, and know that if you properly follow The Recipe, it will not only bring you success in business but also in each of your personal journeys.

We hope that our last gift to you brings you rewards, validation, a sense of purpose, and satisfaction equal to those that we have enjoyed.

We love you all very much and could not be prouder of you.

With all our love,

Mom and Pop

# Chapter 2 - Six Brothers

The words of the Givvantakes hung in the air.

Mary, who had known each of the men since before they could crawl, settled back in her chair and said nothing.

Their parents had named them strong men's names. But having watched them grow up, she had names of her own for them.

Allan, the oldest, always felt his place and had a dash of "*AllAboutMe.*" He was often the first to make changes, to step out front, and to take charge -- whether you asked him to or not. Pop used to tease him. "Boy, be sure your ego doesn't get so big that it enters the room before you do!" Allan would take the good natured ribbing from Pop, but if his brothers dared do it, well, that was another story.

Ivan, who came next, often was the brother to say "*IWantWhatYouHave.*" It was hard for him to stand in his brothers' shadows -- even though, more often than not, he was happiest outside of the spotlight. If he could just learn to appreciate the many gifts he already had, Mary thought, he would be far less worried about what he might be missing.

*The Recipe: A Fable for Leaders and Teams*

Nate's favorite phrase was *"NotMyFault."* The most cautious of the brothers, he was so worried that something might go wrong that he was always the one to try to put everything in to a safe zone - seeking advice from anyone who would share it. He had yet to learn how to trust his own instincts and those of others, so he often looked to place blame before a problem even arose.

Yale's name was *"Yeah, Maybe"* since that was his favorite phrase. Kind and agreeable, he never wanted to be contrary, the way Nate sometimes might be. But still in most discussions he first would agree and then question further, leaving others with the sense of never quite knowing if he were in or out. He was afraid that if he acted too soon he might miss something important.

Oliver, with all of his energy, was a bit *"OverTheTop."* The big idea man, often the life of the party, he always wanted to add the excitement, the flash and the sizzle. Mary knew that the motive behind all of his grand gestures was Oliver's desire to be accepted and viewed as an equal by his brothers.

While Sam, the youngest, struggled to be heard, he always had *"SomethingToSay."* Often what he had to add brought real value, but he was so concerned that no one was listening or paying attention to what he had to offer, that he often tried too hard, and his message got lost in the noise.

*The Recipe: A Fable for Leaders and Teams*

So when they came to Mary's mind -- that's who they were. Each of the six brothers had a personality and gifts that defined him in a way that no simple name ever could.

The silence was quickly broken by Allan. "I am the only one who can run this business. Mom and Pop would want me to be the leader and take charge."

Ivan, not wanting to be outdone by his brother or placed in the second seat, said, "If you can run the bakery, so can I! And anyway, how do you know that Mom and Pop would want you to be the boss?"

Nate just shook his head, smirked and let out a cynical chuckle. "You think all of you can run the bakery? Well, if you guys take this on and mess up the business, you'll drive 50 years of hard work into the ground. It won't be my fault."

As Yale sat watching his brothers, an uncertain look washed over his face. He creased his forehead. "I'm not quite sure how I feel about owning *Prosperous Bakery*," he said. "There is a lot of time and effort involved in running a business like this. Yeah, maybe we should consider selling."

"No worries!" exclaimed Oliver, jumping into the conversation and to his feet. "I'm the perfect one to run *Prosperous Bakery*," he said, pointing at his chest. "I know everyone. I can make it more profitable… I can build another one! …. I bet we can even start a franchise!"

Sam sat back in his chair with his arms crossed, listening as his brothers jockeyed for position. "Uh hum." He cleared his throat to get their attention. "After listening to all of you voice your ideas, thoughts and opinions, I have something to say. I highly suggest we take a vote to determine who will be in charge. It's what we should do, and what makes the best sense if we are to continue *Prosperous Bakery* in a way that Mom and Pop would want."

The tension grew as the six brothers squabbled back and forth about who should be in charge of *Prosperous Bakery*.

Each of them had fond memories of working in the bakery alongside Mom and Pop while growing up, and felt his time working there made him the right one to lead.

Mary recalled that although it had taken hard work and long hours, the Givvantakes had a knack for making it come together and having fun along the way.

Over the years they had developed the ability, talent and foresight to make the business successful. For each of the brothers, working in *Prosperous Bakery* had been an important part of who they were and who they had become over the years. Mary also knew that who they were had been shaped by the time they had spent with the Givvantakes.

She recalled Mom and Pop Givvantake's special talent for really seeing people and for bringing out the best in them. In the case of their grandsons, they had known what each man's talents were, as well as what their challenges would be. During their lives, the Givvantakes had been a guide to the brothers. Now, Mary thought to herself, that role will be mine as they take their next steps along life's journey.

Mary knew the six brothers were not the only ones who had great respect and admiration for the Givvantakes or the special place *Prosperous Bakery* held in the heart of the town. It was home to the people that worked there, to the customers who came in for something special, and a gathering spot for the community. *Prosperous Bakery* was an important part of their lives. It was more than just a bake shop or one family's business. Mary had learned from Mom and Pop that people connect by shared experiences. It was their job to make *Prosperous Bakery* provide the place for shared experiences and great memories.

Mary had worked in *Prosperous Bakery* for close to fifty years. She remembered when Johnny Thompson proposed to Millie at the corner table and how, to this day, he always comes in to pick up a special cake for their anniversary. Many groups, ranging from the Girls Scouts to the Garden Club, all met around the big oak table in the back room. It was the place where Toastmasters came weekly to fine tune their presentation skills, and it was a favorite hangout for the high school kids when classes let out. Their parents had never worried about where they were. They knew that Mom and Pop were there to keep an eye on things. *Prosperous Bakery* was everyone's place and an important part of so many of the good things in their lives.

She let the boys ramble on, listening as they argued and then moved on to talk about the good times by sharing their numerous stories. They miss the Givvantakes, she thought to herself. Their grandparents have been such a big part of their lives, not to mention all of ours. She let them run on for a bit more. Then she got up from the table. The brothers ceased their banter as she began to speak.

"This has been quite a day for all of us. Why don't we all continue this discussion tomorrow? Can you please meet me here for coffee again in the morning? I'll bring you scones tomorrow," she said, with a glance at the six cardboard cups from the gas station that were still sitting on the table, "and even make the coffee."

The brothers agreed, and after giving Mary a hug, each went on his way. The little bells chimed as the door opened and closed behind them.

With a sad little sigh, Mary looked around a now quiet *Prosperous Bakery*. Then she went back to the Community Room to clear away the plates, silverware, and six empty cardboard coffee cups. She loaded them on her tray and took the dishes into the kitchen to place in the dish washer. Then she went back into the Community Room to get her purse and the now smaller stack of envelopes from Mom and Pop

On her way out, she stopped at the door and took one last look around. Everything was quiet and in its place once again.

"Well, Mom and Pop," she said to the now quiet store.

"We have a bit of mixing and baking to do. But I'm sure this batch will come out fine. After all, you left me your treasures and *The Recipe* for them in my keeping."

With that, she shut off the lights.

The little bells jingled as she walked out the door and put her key in the door to lock things up all safe and sound.

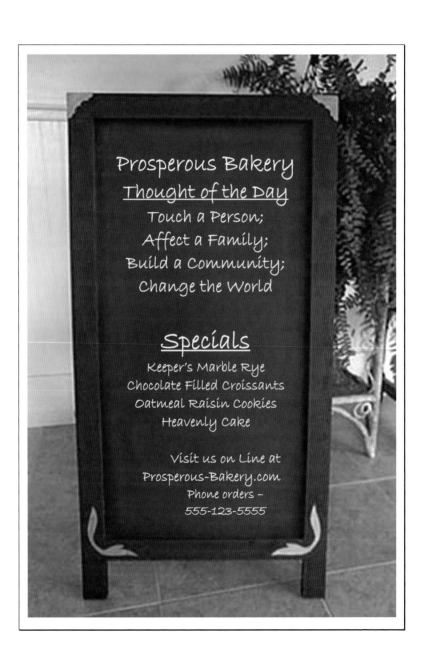

# Chapter 3 - Mary

The next morning, as the brothers wandered into the Community Room one at a time, Mary greeted each of them with a hug and a question about their wives, children or friends.

When they all had arrived, she began to speak. "Everyone will be so happy to see all of you again, and they'll be pleased to see that *Prosperous Bakery* will continue keeping true to the longstanding traditions that were established by Mom and Pop. If you will just make yourself comfortable, I need to help the crew get started and will be with you in a few minutes." She then went back to check in with the counter crew.

It was a busy morning at *Prosperous Bakery*. The line of customers stretched out the door as it did most every day. Customers passed the time with greetings, and chatted with one another as they patiently waited to place their order. Most of the tables were filled with guests enjoying their food and each other's company.

Right in the mix of it all was Mary - from greeting and serving customers to making sure the kitchen, café, and counter crews had what they needed, Mary was perfectly in tune with the business. The brothers watched as she oversaw everything and missed nothing. All was running smoothly. It was as if nothing had changed, and the Givvantakes were still there.

The boys had grown up watching their grandparents build the bakery, from a small storefront run by just the two of them, to a bakery café with a team of many that was open daily from 6 AM to 6 PM.

*Prosperous Bakery* had survived hard economic times, the coming of chain stores, an ever-changing workforce, new trends in the community, and the many other challenges that face any growing business. Together, with their team, they had faced each one. Where other businesses failed, *Prosperous Bakery* continued to hold its place in the community as everyone's favorite bake shop and gathering place.

From the open double doors of the Community Room, the brothers watched as Mary, with a friendly smile and clear efficiency, kept the line moving and the customers smiling. When things were down to the last of the morning rush, Mary came back out from behind the counter to join them in the doorway.

"You never cease to amaze me, Mary," said Sam in his best *SomethingToSay* voice as she approached. "No matter how busy it is or how long the wait, you always have them leaving happy."

"It's not me. It's our team," she replied. "The Givvantakes shaped us into a great team. There was nothing they would not do for a good customer or a good employee and they encouraged us to be the same way. Mom and Pop even had a card by the register to remind us that read:

> *'It easier to keep a good customer…*
> *It's harder to find a new one.'*

They were our champions, our leaders, our friends. Every one of us knew what we could expect from them AND what was expected of us. It was not just good business. It was a way of living your life and caring for others. We mattered to them and we knew it. They did not always say it. Instead, they showed us in many different ways. Because of that, they mattered to us, too."

They were all still gathered in the doorway chatting when Mrs. Birdway from the Garden Club entered the shop to the tinkling of bells, and waved at Mary.

"I'll try to make this quick. I'm sure she just wants to chat for a minute about the Garden Club event next week," Mary said, as she left to go speak to one the of the bakery's long time customers.

"No one can chat with Mrs. Birdway for a MINUTE," said Allan, stepping forward. "She can talk your ear off."

"Yeah," chimed in Yale. "And maybe ask you a million personal questions you DON'T want to answer," he said with a shudder, moving forward to stand next to his older brother.

"Or pinch your cheeks," added Sam. "The last time I saw here she was pinching my cheeks and making a fuss. I was out on a date with Nancy and it was awful. Nancy kept saying it was adorable, which only made it worse. She was so busy laughing that she did not listen to a word I was saying."

"Oooh, you're sooo cute," joked Oliver in his best falsetto, reaching out to pinch his baby brother's cheeks with both hands. Before Sam could hit him, Allan jumped between the two.

"Enough already," he said. "Pay attention, you guys. Mrs. Birdwell is NOT talking Mary's ear off. Old Lady Birdwell is listening AND taking notes. I've never seen anything like it."

"Yeah, maybe Mary knows something about working with Mrs. Birdwell that we don't," said Yale, thoughtfully.

"Or maybe Mary has a secret trick to keep her from talking so much," said Ivan. "Wish I could do that. Mary seems to know how to make Mrs. Birdwell listen instead of just fluttering back and forth from one subject to the next. Mary gets her to listen and give her all of her attention without doing anything special. I want whatever Mary has that makes people do that, whatever it is."

*The Recipe: A Fable for Leaders and Teams*

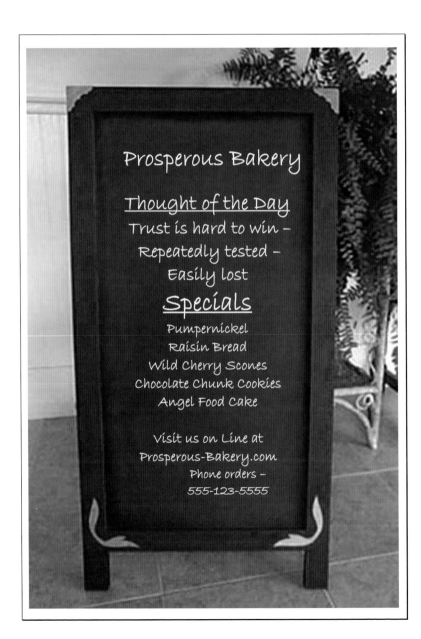

# Chapter 4 – Mixing It Up

They watched as Mary led Mrs. Birdwell to one of the café tables and then went behind the counter to get her a cup of tea and a crumpet. None of the brothers had to guess about that order. Mrs. Birdwell had been having the same thing every time she came into the bakery, even back in the days when they had each worked there during their high school summer vacations.

Once she was comfortably settled with her treat, Mary came back to join them in the doorway.

"Oh, my," she said. "I hope I did not take too long. Mrs. Birdwell is such a dear, and I wanted to make sure she was happy with all of next week's arrangements."

"Is the Garden Club doing something new and different?" asked Oliver eagerly. "I was just thinking that it's about time to liven things up a bit. We can make it more festive around here, and drum up even more business. An event for the Garden Club would be a great time to start."

"No," replied Mary. "Everything is the same and the ladies like it that way. It is just that Mrs. Birdwell takes her responsibilities as chairwoman of the Garden Club very seriously and she wanted to be sure everything would be ready.

"But why does she have to monitor something if nothing is changing?" asked Allan. "You would think after all these years she would know it will be ready, especially if nothing has changed."

"The monthly meeting is a special time for the ladies," explained Mary. "She always stops in to make sure everything is set. It's paying attention to the little details that makes a person feel special and helps to ensure a great event and repeat business. For many of our customers and our people too, they get a sense of security and stability from our paying attention to the tiniest of details. I'm always happy to see her and to make the time to go over things. It helps keep me on my toes and neither of us takes anything for granted. I just was not expecting her so early today."

Mary and the men moved into the Community Room where a tray of fresh scones and a thermal carafe of coffee sat in the center. Like the day before, Mary went to the sideboard and got out the serving pieces and cups and brought them to the table.

"Now, let's get started," Mary said, as she passed out the coffee cups and plates. "Do any of you have any questions that you thought of since we talked yesterday?"

"I have everything under control, Mary," said Allan with confidence. "After all, I've worked here for years off and on. Of course, I can always make improvements, but as the oldest, I'm the logical one to be in charge. You can trust me to know what to do and I'll be sure to let you know when I change something to make it better."

"Hold on, Bro'," exclaimed Ivan. "Who died and made YOU boss?"

"Now THAT was tactful," injected Nate with a wince. "Mom and Pop left *Prosperous Bakery* to all of us equally. We've all worked here since we were kids, anyway. No one is "The Boss" here. We're all in this together and I for one think we need to have a plan. Like I said yesterday – this is a big responsibility and you guys better not screw it up..."

Here we go again, thought Mary. This batch is having a bit of a challenge holding together.

It's like making bread dough. You need to mix it well, knead it until it holds together, then let it rest and give it time to rise before you expose it to the heat of the oven. No need to rush it now.

As she watched and listened to each brother state his case, the volume in the room began to rise.

Now this won't do, she thought to herself. Mom and Pop would never disagree so loudly that our customers or employees could hear. Perhaps it is time to step in and remind them.

"Gentlemen," Mary said in her quiet voice. But there was no response. The men were still fully focused on talking over each other and did not seem to hear her. "Gentlemen," she began again as she rose from her seat at the table to get their attention. "You might want to remember that we have customers out front, not to mention our team…. Do you ever remember your grandparents raising their voices or arguing with each other where others could hear?"

"Yeah, guys, keep it down," said Nate as he moved to look through the doorway.

"I'll handle it," said Allan. "I know what needs to be done. Not a problem. Anyway we've wasted too much time talking – all this idle chatter is not getting us anywhere – I have work to do and a bakery to run. You guys can wrap it up here with Mary. I have more important things to do. Just fill me in later." With that, he brushed by Mary and hurried out the door and over towards the counter.

"Mary," asked Ivan "Mom and Pop left us the bakery. But what did you get? I did not hear anything about you when they read the will. I mean we're family and all. It makes sense the bakery came to us, but you've been here forever. What did you get?"

"They left me some letters," she replied, patting her bag, "and something else very special to me, just as they left each of you something special in *Prosperous Bakery* and *The Recipe*. I'm happy with my gifts. They actually gave them to me long ago, so I did not need anything more now."

Nate was staring down at his legal pad, adding to what he had already written down at the reading of the will. "We all need to go over the terms of the will again soon with the lawyers. There may be something we missed. I don't know about you, but I certainly don't want to have fingers pointing at me if we overlook something big and something goes wrong with the business."

Yale stood back and watched. He still wasn't sure what to think. Questions kept running through his mind – the same ones that had kept him up all night the night before. "I wonder if owning *Prosperous Bakery* is really a good thing." He just didn't know. "Are we in over our heads? Can we make a go of it?"

And as unsure as Yale was, Oliver was watching the lunch crowd begin to wander in, getting more excited by the minute. "Come on, Come on. Let's get out there – it's almost time for the lunch rush. Let's crank up the energy, and turn up the music. This place will be hoppin' in a few minutes. It's time to get out there." he said, leaving the room to hurry over to the old jukebox in the corner.

Following his brothers out of the room, Sam began moving around to the tables, greeting old customers and meeting new ones. He knew he had as much to offer as any of his brothers and he was not about to be left behind or be overlooked. He had something to say to make everyone feel welcome.

Mary remained standing back in the doorway of the Community Room, watching and listening.

They're all so worried, she thought with a smile. Each is going in a different direction. Oh, my, now all six of them have stopped by Mayor Maloney's table to say hello. The poor man will never get to finish his lunch.

Making her way back to the table, Mary again gathered up the plates and empty cups. Taking them into the kitchen, she saw Joe, now the head baker since Pop was gone. He was carefully setting the next batch of loaves in the rack to rise.

"Everything OK out there?" he asked.

"It will be soon," Mary answered. "Everything's in the mix, it will just take a bit more time before it all comes together."

"Pop always told me… you just mix it up, knead it a bit, and then give it time to rise," Joe said. "That's how you bake a great batch."

"That he did," Mary said with a smile, glancing up at the needlepoint sampler Mom had stitched years ago. Pop had proudly hung in his kitchen. It  read...

> *Touch a Person*
> *Affect a Family*
> *Build a Community*
> *Change the World*

 Mary watched from the kitchen pass-through as the brothers continued to move around the tables. Yes, she thought, a bit of kneading is what we need now.  We have all the right ingredients

Sometimes how you mix the ingredients makes all the difference in the world. Sometimes you beat it up with lots of urgency. Other times you mix it gently by hand.  It takes just the right touch to make it all come out right, not to tough, but not too flaky that it can't hold together.

It's funny, she thought. They all want to be sure that their position and ownership is secure, but not one of them has asked about *The Recipe*. Yet *The Recipe* is the secret to what makes *Prosperous Bakery* so successful.

She could not help but smile. So often what we are looking for is close at hand. We just can't see it until we are ready to. Just like Mom and Pop often said, "As much as you might like to rush or take a shortcut in the baking process, you might end up with something nobody wants to eat."

Once you have chosen the right ingredients you are only half way there. The rest is following the steps and adding the right amount of energy at the right time so you can get the best results.

The Givvantakes knew that, and so did the bakery employees. Perhaps the boys had just forgotten about it since things have been so stirred up with all the changes.

Mom and Pop built *Prosperous Bakery* based on a community of WE but the boys were still focused individually on ME.

It was like her favorite cookie recipe. You need the finest flour, the creamiest butter, and the freshest eggs. But it is not until you blend them together and bake them in the oven that you get something truly delightful.

### Little Spoonfuls

To learn more about Mary's secret ingredients for creating and sustaining trust, see the Little Spoonfuls Appendix.

# Chapter 5 – Today's Menu

At the end of the day as the counter staff was ringing up the last of the customers and the wait staff cleared the last of the café tables, Mary called the brothers back into the now quiet kitchen.

There, on Joe's spotless baker's table, sat a selection of different cookies. Mary believed the comfort of the kitchen with its familiar surroundings would be the perfect place for this next discussion.

Once each brother had selected his favorite cookie, Mary said brightly, "I can't wait to hear what you boys have planned for *Prosperous Bakery*. It's been at the center of the family for years and an integral part of the community. Have you decided what you want to do now that *Prosperous Bakery* is yours?"

One by one, the brothers began to tell Mary a small bit of their plans for the bakery, each angling to get her stamp of approval.

Allan, as the eldest, was the first to speak. True to form, he gave a long list of all the changes he thought necessary to take the bakery forward. He included everything from renaming it to creating a new menu. Verbally he sketched out his ideas about new décor, new signage and he even had named one of the pastries after himself.   And, of course, his title should be Chief Executive Officer since he would be overseeing the entire operation, with everyone reporting directly to him.

Oliver looked at Allan, and then at Mary and his other siblings. "Did I miss something? When was he elected CEO?  I can make things even better. I have GREAT ideas." Then he began ticking off a list of all the changes that he would make. He concluded with, "I can make the bakery more profitable than Mom and Pop ever imagined."

It was like a flag had dropped between the two brothers and they were off.  Each began arguing why he would make the best leader for *Prosperous Bakery*. They were so focused on topping each other's ideas that they were oblivious to Mary and the other brothers in the room.

Sam was not about to be left out of the discussion. "This is why I said we should have taken a vote about who should be in charge, and what we should do. You should have listened to me. But, you guys NEVER listen to me," he said, turning his back on his brothers and walking over to lean against the now empty baker's rack.

"We always hear you. You never shut up!" joked Oliver.

"Why are you guys acting as if the rest of us are not here? We're all owners, too. Why should any of you be in charge? If you can do it, so can I." Not liking this at all, Ivan pushed away from the baker's table. He moved over by the sink where he leaned back and crossed his arms.

Mary glanced around the room, then turned to Yale and asked if he had something to add. "I need more data," he answered. "We need to study this. It's too soon to make any big changes. I need to research things more and so do you all of you," he continued, turning to look around the room at his brothers. "*Prosperous Bakery* has been the same for years and it's successful. Before we make changes, we need to think things through. These might all be great ideas, but we need to observe and make decisions after we know a little more. I don't feel comfortable moving this quickly."

While all this was going on, Nate had been madly jotting down notes. "This is a big responsibility," he said, looking up from his pad. "We need to call in the experts. I know a consulting firm full of specialists that we can bring in to evaluate how we do everything and tell us what is best. That way we won't make any mistakes. I know some. They are the professionals. Bringing them in is what we need to do first. They can do the research, document the processes, and help us shape the vision. Then, when we are ready, we need to map out every move."

Mary listened as the brothers continued to bicker. Each one had his own idea of what needed to be done next, yet was paying little attention to what any of the others had to say. As the conversation continued, it seemed like each was becoming more and more stuck on his own ideas or cemented to a position. They had even spread further apart, moving around the kitchen and raising their voices to be heard.

Finally, Mary reached into the drawer of the baker's table and pulled out a big wooden spoon. Rapping it against the table to get their attention, she said calmly, "All of you have taken your role as new owners very seriously, which I know would make Mom and Pop proud. Here is an idea that might move us forward. It is also clear that each of you has your own approach and thoughts as to what is best for the future of the bakery. What if each of you takes a turn to run the business for a day? Then we can see which plans, and whose ideas and talents, are best suited for leading *Prosperous Bakery*. You could each have a day to demonstrate your ideas and then come back together at the end of the week to agree on what worked best. We could start next Monday with each of you having your day. That should give each of you some time to prepare. In the meantime, the crew can continue on as we have until now. Then after a week where you each take a turn as the leader, we can come back together at my cottage on that Saturday night, after we close. We'll be away from the eyes and ears of the staff and the customers. You can work through it all and decide what you want to do going forward."

For once, the brothers all agreed. Each was thinking "this will be my opportunity to shine and clearly demonstrate to my brothers that it will be in *Prosperous Bakery's* best interest to do things my way."

As they hurried away to make their plans, Mary gathered up the empty plate of cookies, wiped down the kitchen counters, turned off the kitchen lights, and made her way to the doors to lock up.

Passing the Welcome Station, she looked over at the picture of the Givvantakes surrounded by the smiling *Prosperous Bakery* crew that had been taken last Christmas and hung by Pop with pride on the wall.

What a team they had made, she thought to herself. Each member of the crew knew just where they fit, what to do, and, most of the time, how to do it. And when they needed help, Mom and Pop had always been there with a suggestion, a helping hand, a smile or a pat on the back.

"Well, Mom and Pop," she said as she turned off the last of the lights. "Next week should be an interesting week."

With a jingle of bells, Mary passed through the door of *Prosperous Bakery*, turned her key in the lock, and headed home for the night.

### Little Spoonfuls

To learn more about Mary's secret ingredients for addressing conflict and building consensus see the Little Spoonfuls Appendix.

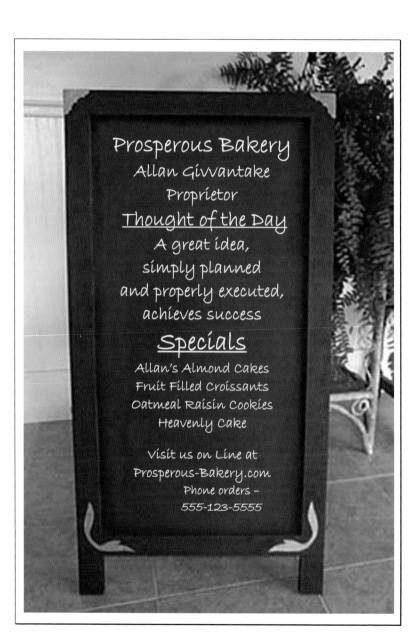

# Chapter 6 - Monday

This was the Big Week. It was time for the new owners to each take a turn as the leader of *Prosperous Bakery*.

When his brothers arrived bright and early Monday morning, Allan was already there and the changes already had begun.

A sign hung from the door with a big color picture of Allan that read:

> **Under NEW Management**
>
> **Allan Givvantake, Proprietor**

Shocked at his boldness, the other five brothers entered the bakery to find Allan at the chalk board menu replacing some items on the menu with his personal favorites, deleting others that had always been dependable best sellers, and, of course, adding his signature product – Allan's Almond Cakes.

Instead of having a hostess greeting the customers, a life-sized cardboard cut-out of you-know-who stood at the door.

With the crew all together in the café, Allan began to hold his first morning meeting.

"It's a new day at *Prosperous Bakery,* and we have lots to do," he told them all as he passed out sheets of paper filled with tightly spaced words, stapled at the top. "Here is a list of the changes I want made. Be sure to read it. And be sure to run all questions and decisions by me. I know you all have been here for years, but *Prosperous Bakery* is now under new management. You'll see. Things will be better than ever before."

The crew looked at the long list of things to do. Some of them smiled, while others just nodded their heads. Then they went off to their stations and prepared for opening.

Mary smiled as she watched the crew take their places. They were a good team, she thought to herself, and they wanted to impress the "new boss." Working with the Givvantakes had taught them to be open and receptive to new ideas.

Mary recognized the value of bringing in innovative ideas and knew that Allan had lots of energy. He was passionate about making *Prosperous Bakery* bigger and better. But, she thought, sometimes a little can go a long way. I hope he isn't trying to do too much too fast.

*The Recipe: A Fable for Leaders and Teams*

But as the day went on that was just what started to happen. There were a lot of changes on that list and they were just changes, not instructions on actually how to do it. Some of the changes were unclear and needed more explanation.

As the employees stopped at each task to report or consult with Allan, the easy flow of *Prosperous Bakery* came to a stuttering halt. The soothing comfort and the ambience that made both the employees and customers happy to be there began to evaporate.

The counter team was not efficient as it usually was, and the line was taking forever.

If something was not on the list, somebody had to find the boss before they could make a decision, and while they looked for Allan, the customers waited.

All these new names for old favorites and too many choices confused the customers, and slowed down the counter crew.

There was no cheerful banter in the line this Monday morning. Regulars kept looking at their watches, grumbling about being late for work. The staff kept checking "the list" under Allan's watchful eye. And each time they did, things got a little slower. Mary saw that the crew's rhythm was gone. And as hard as they were trying, they just could not seem to get it back.

Allan was hoping that as the day went on things would get better, but everything seemed to be getting worse.

Joe and the kitchen crew were in a snit because no one had told them to order more ingredients for the new items on the menu, so they kept running out of what they needed.

When the lunch rush started, there was nobody at the Welcome Station to usher people in. A life-sized cardboard cutout could not answer customers' questions about the new menu items, or find them a table. Many simply moved on down the street to grab lunch somewhere else.

And where are my brothers, complained Allan to himself. They were offering no help at all. All morning they just sat at the café table towards the back, watching the chaos with looks of horror on their faces.

Not one of them offered to help out – and no way am I going to ask them, Allan fumed.

At one point, at the height of the lunch rush, Allan had stopped by his brothers' table to point out that several customers were waiting. Instead of pitching in to help, his brothers just gathered up their stuff and moved to the Community Room. They did not even clear their own table. He had to do it himself!

Mary could see that Allan was frustrated at the end of his day. He was feeling undermined by the lack of support from his brothers and the continuing confusion of *Prosperous Bakery's* crew.

He did have great ideas, she thought looking down at the list he had given her at the beginning of the day, but he had not done a great job communicating how the tasks should be accomplished.

His brothers had left earlier, shaking their heads. Each was thinking his own thoughts of how "their day" would be better.

As the afternoon crew began the process of closing up, Mary went over to the corner café table where Allan sat alone with his list of ideas.

"How are you feeling about your day?" She asked quietly as she sat down beside him.

"Lousy," he said, gazing down at the list in his hand. "If only everyone had done what I told them to do. It would have been great. All they had to do was make a few little changes. It was not like I assigned them all new jobs or anything. Not a single one could just follow my instructions. Everybody kept asking for more and more direction. My

*The Recipe: A Fable for Leaders and Teams*

brothers were no help at all. They just sat there watching and waiting for me to crash and burn. It was chaos!"

"If you could do it all again, what would you do differently?" Mary asked, as she took the list from his hand and set it on the table.

"Let's look at your list. You have some great ideas here," she said pointing to the items on the paper. "But you need to keep in mind that some of the team may not be quite as quick in adapting to new things as you are. It's not that they don't want to help. They're just not sure how. They might need more explanation, or more time to process new information so they can figure out how to make it work for them. Not everyone can just see it and do it like you do. Some people need examples to go by, and others need to learn things hands on.

The crew was eager to work with you and help. They just did not know exactly what you needed them to do, and it threw them off their stride."

"Yeah, then one thing led to another and before you know it – CRASH!"

"Now it wasn't that bad" she said. "Come on, Boss Man, I'll help you close up. You've had a long day."

So that Monday night, a team of two again closed up shop at *Prosperous Bakery*. In the end, Mary stood by the door with her keys while Allan got the lights.

The little bells jingled as out they went, and he walked Mary down the street to her car.

### Little Spoonfuls

Dealing with change is a fact of life for leaders and teams.

See the Little Spoonfuls Appendix for insights into dealing with change.

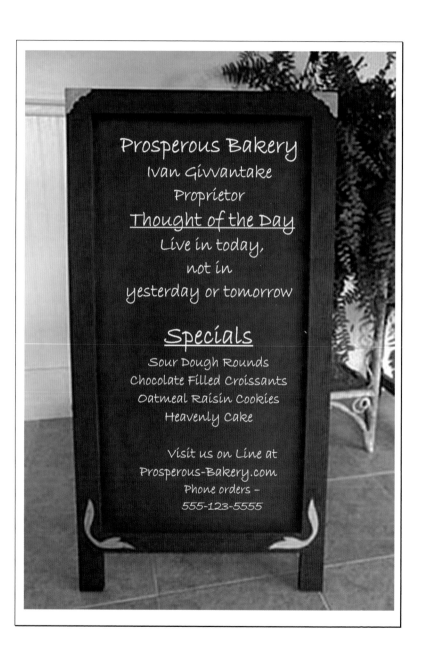

# Chapter 7 - Tuesday

On Tuesday it was Ivan's turn to take charge of the bakery.
The first order of business was to take down his brother's
sign and replace it with one of his own that read:

> **Welcome!**
>
> **Under NEW Management**
>
> **Ivan Givvantake, Proprietor**

He took what his brothers had jokingly named Cardboard
Allan under his arm and carried the cut-out into the storage
room. There he propped it up on the wall behind the mops
and the buckets. Then he went back out front and placed
some pictures of himself and his family on the wall behind
the welcome station, right next to the photo of his
grandparents and the crew from last year's Christmas Party.

Allan blew it with the cut-out, Ivan thought to himself. I get
that people what to know who's in charge, but you don't
have to be so blatant about it.

He stepped back to look and see if the pictures were straight
and nodded his approval.

These photographs are just the right touch, he thought to himself. It leaves my mark, and gives the place a nice homey feel.

"OK," he said to himself. "Next stop the menu."

Going to the chalk board that listed the items of the day, he removed many of the new items Allan had added yesterday, replacing them with *Prosperous Bakery's* standard fare, yet leaving one or two that he actually had liked for further testing. Then, for that little extra, he added one or two specials of his own. He planned to offer samples of the new menu options to customers throughout the day and gather their opinions.

Opening the door to the morning crew, Ivan asked the staff to join him in the café section.

Not surprisingly his brothers and Mary where there, too. Mary took her place with the crew while his brothers clustered around the corner table.

"OK, let's get started," Ivan said with an air of authority. "Many of you have worked here for years. You know your jobs and how to do them. I want you to do what you do best. We'll get things back to normal with just a little taste of change," he said, pointing to the chalk board behind the

*The Recipe: A Fable for Leaders and Teams*

counter. He smiled when he noticed that the kitchen crew looked relieved.

"Joe, would you please make up some sample trays of these new bakery items? I want to get some input from the customers as they wait this morning and see what they think."

"Mary, could you please hang around with the counter and café crew to make sure that the line keeps moving? We don't need another backup like yesterday. Sorry, Allan. If you need me, I will be at the welcome station."

As the crews went to their stations, Ivan was pretty happy with himself.

Now they'll see how a real leader does it, he thought, as he reviewed his plans for the day. With everything in place, he was ready to go. At long last, he was not just Allan's younger brother. He was in charge and he knew exactly what he wanted to do. As he had said to his wife just this morning, "This is MY day and it's going to be a great one."

At the corner café table, the brothers looked at Allan. How was he taking all this?

"You OK, Allan?" asked Sam as he laid a hand on Allan's arm.

"Yesterday was a killer." Allan replied. "We'll see how Ivan does today. He's always wanted to be number one. Now this is his chance. It's nice to see that he at least kept some of my ideas. We'll have to see what he can do with them."

"Wonder what he did with Cardboard Allan?" asked Sam.

"Ugh, don't remind me. Looking back, even I know that idea may have been a bit over the top."

"Hey, that's my line…" said Oliver, as they all laughed.

Hearing the laughter from the corner table, Mary saw Ivan straighten his shoulders. Here we go, she thought, as the morning coffee crowd began to line up.

Throughout the day, Mary watched as Ivan went about the business of running *Prosperous Bakery*.

Even with things back to normal, there were always a million things to do: lots of interruptions, customers looking for conversation, and those little things the crew needs help with that always pop up, even on the best of days.

She saw Ivan glowing from the positive feedback he was getting from customers when he offered free samples of some of the new menu items. And thankfully, the crew was getting back their rhythm as things returned to a routine that they were more used to.

But Mary noticed other things, too. She knew that being out in front all day long can take a toll on some people. By the end of the lunch rush she suspected that Ivan had started to drag a bit. The enthusiasm of the morning now was gone and his tone had grown sterner. After lunch was over, he spent most of the afternoon back in the kitchen with Joe, or back in the quiet of the office with the bookkeeper who was balancing the prior day's receipts.

As the day came to a close, his brothers were gone, the bookkeeper was finished, and the kitchen crew had said their goodbyes. Mary was sitting at a café table resting her feet when he came to join her. It had been a long time since she had spent so much time behind the counter, too, and it made for a long day for her old feet.

"So how do you think it went?" she asked, as he pulled his chair up to the table.

"OK, I guess. The customers liked the free samples and I got some great feedback. But I felt like someone always wanted a piece of me, too." He settled back in his chair. "You know, I always wanted to be up front and center stage like Allan and the others. But now that I've been there…"

"It was not quite like you imagined, then?" Mary asked.

"I thought it would be great, but by the end of the day, I just wanted to find a quiet corner. I am exhausted. Things went pretty well, but it's only been one day and dealing with all those people, questions, and constant interruptions takes a lot out of you. I don't want to let anyone down, but all in all, I finally realize I'm much happier behind the scenes. The rest of the guys can have it. It's just not for me."

"You're not letting anyone down," said Mary as she patted his hand. "It takes a strong person to recognize what they're best at. When anyone tries to be something or someone they are not, it sucks out all of your energy. You can fake it for a while, but eventually something has to give."

"Each of us works best when we use our natural talents," she continued. "Plus, knowing what comes less naturally to you is equally important. It gives you the chance to reach out and work with others who have different talents and strengths to help you. What you learned about yourself today does not make you less of a leader. It makes you a better one."

"Thanks, Mary. I really mean that. Things would not have gone as well today without you out front helping me. I noticed and I appreciate it." Ivan reached over to give her a hug. "Are you ready to call it a day?"

And so they did. Together, they finished closing up
*Prosperous Bakery.*

He opened the door to the jingling of the bells and held it
for Mary. "After you, madam," he said with a smile, as he
followed her out into the night, and walked her to her car.

### Little Spoonfuls

Awareness can be one of a leader's
greatest tools.

See the Little Spoonfuls Appendix
for insights into how to increase
awareness in your team.

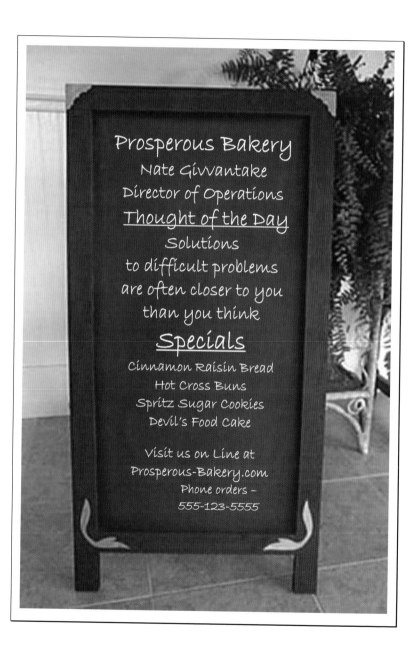

Prosperous Bakery
Nate Givvantake
Director of Operations
<u>Thought of the Day</u>
Solutions
to difficult problems
are often closer to you
than you think
## <u>Specials</u>
Cinnamon Raisin Bread
Hot Cross Buns
Spritz Sugar Cookies
Devil's Food Cake

Visit us on Line at
Prosperous-Bakery.com
Phone orders –
555-123-5555

# Chapter 8 - Wednesday

As Wednesday dawned, Nate gathered up folders full of his meticulously typed up notes and graphs and made his way to *Prosperous Bakery*. Taking his key from his pocket he opened the door, placed the folders inside, and then went back to the car to get his easels, charts and his own sign for the front window.

---

**Welcome!**

**Under NEW Management**

**Nate Givvantake, Head of Operations**

---

Nate knew something that he believed his brothers did not. Solutions to difficult problems are often right before your eyes. You just need to pay attention and look for them.

He always tried to pay attention to details, calculate the odds, test his projections, and look for the efficiencies. To his mind, that is how you build a great business.

Nate was certain that problems did not just happen by chance. They were caused by not paying attention to the signs you could find by looking at the details. *Prosperous*

*Bakery* was going to be MORE prosperous because he knew what to look for.

At exactly 4 AM he opened the door to Joe and the kitchen crew. "Joe, you and the team are excused from the morning meeting in the café. Here are the things I want you to focus on and the order they should happen in," he said, handing him a flow chart  that had been laminated to prevent it from being damaged by little kitchen mishaps. "You will see that I have followed your morning routine with some minor changes to increase the efficiency and the flow.  The first set of items should be moved from the racks to the shelves at exactly 5:45, so we will be ready when the doors open at 6 AM."

Joe just stared at the list and then back at Nate.  The kitchen had been his domain for over 20 years and he did not need anyone to tell him what to put in his ovens and when.  "I really appreciate your suggestions, but if I prep things in this order some of the items won't be fresh for the main rush at 7.  Are you sure this is what you want?" Joe asked.

"Just try it, and then mark down any needed adjustments on the chart so we can review them later," Nate said, as he pulled a special red marker from his pocket and handed it to Joe.  "I will be out in the café getting things ready for the meeting with the rest of the crew.  You can find me there if you have any questions."

As Nate headed back out to the café area, Joe walked to the store room to get his supplies for the day. If the bag of flour hit his baker's table a bit harder than normal, there was no one else around to notice. Nate means well, thought Joe, but I probably know more about my kitchen than a newbie who used to be my kitchen helper. But he's a Givvantake. I'll give him a chance.

In the café area, Nate set up a series of charts and flows to explain his ideas to the café and counter crew. Moving between the tables, he used tape to mark where each table should stay positioned for maximum efficiency as the servers would move through them with their orders. Then he moved to the welcome station to take down his brother's family pictures, and then add a sign of his own to the wall.

Help Us Make *Prosperous Bakery* Better.

Submit your suggestion here.

On the desk at the Welcome Station, he set out a wooden suggestion box, a stack of comment cards, and a container of pens that each had *Prosperous Bakery*, its website and a phone number printed on them in gold.

Nate looked down at the gold watch Mom and Pop had given him when he got his MBA a few years back. Just then, the little bells jingled over the front door.

"Ah, Mary, you are right on-time. Did the crew get my memo reminding them that we had an early meeting this morning?"

"Yes, they'll be here," she replied. "It looks like you've been busy. What are all of these charts?"

"Glad you asked," he answered, glowing with pride. "These charts show every aspect of how *Prosperous Bakery* operates. I have analyzed the flow and noted suggestions of where we can increase efficiency and save money. Plus these suggestions will make the work easier for the crew so we can get more done."

Nate went on to explain each chart, showing Mary how they could save money on coffee by filling the cup ¾ of an inch less full to make room for the cream, carefully measuring pie slices with a template to get an extra slice out of each pie, and a new service flow for the kitchen and the café.

As he was finishing up, his brothers and the morning crew came in. Again he explained his philosophy and the need for data and analysis, walking them all through every chart, and explaining what he expected of them.

Closing his presentation, he said, "You all know me. I'm not an out-in-front kind of guy like my brothers. Instead I'll be right behind you watching and taking notes. We are back to business as usual. The old menu is back so you do not have any surprises you'll need to work around, and there is a suggestion box at the Welcome Station so that you and the customers can share your ideas for improvements. You know *Prosperous Bakery*, and I know how to make it even better. Just do what you do. I'll be watching."

As the crew took their opening positions, Nate picked up his easels and charts and moved them into the Community Room for a second presentation to the afternoon crew at 10:45.

Then he was back out front, notebook in hand, to watch and observe. And observe he did. Going from the kitchen to the café and to the counter, he spent his day watching everything, taking notes, and making minor adjustments to the flow charts he had created. No detail was too small, and if he did not know the answer, he asked the crew.

He means well, observed Mary to herself as she watched him, but he is making them all crazy, not to mention really nervous, with him always popping up and looking over their shoulders.

Even the most seasoned employees began to question their simplest tasks. They were losing their rhythm again and the customers noticed. Things were not flowing so smoothly as usual, with lines getting longer, and tempers beginning to flare. It was intimidating for Suzie and some of the other counter girls to have someone looking over their shoulders and questioning everything they did. She wanted to be a team player but Suzie was beginning to feel cornered or trapped when everything she did was corrected or questioned.

"Mornings used to be a happy time," she thought. "It was a time when I could help everybody start their day with a coffee and smile, but today I am running out of smiles."

Mary was heading back into the kitchen to take her mid-day break with Joe. As she passed Nate in the doorway she noticed that he looked a bit agitated. "How's it going?" she asked. "Fine, fine, I need to get out to the café to check some things," he said, scurrying past her. As she entered the kitchen she could sense that the atmosphere was not quite the same.

Before she even had time to ask what was up, she came face to face with an angry Joe.

"Mary, you have to do something. If BIG BROTHER stands over my shoulder with that clip board one more time I am going to chop it up and feed it to him! The only peace we've had all day was when he hauled the afternoon crew into the Community Room to for their crew meeting."

Mary spent the next 15 minutes calming down the kitchen crew before heading back to monitor the counter and the café.

She noticed the tension there as well. Everything was running at high efficiency, but the family-friendly feel was missing. The counter banter with customers had all but disappeared, and nobody on the team was smiling.

In the café, customers did not linger like they often did to read the paper, or to visit from table to table.

*Prosperous Bakery* might be getting more efficient, Mary thought, but it was losing its charm and appeal.

She glanced up at the clock over the counter – just a few more hours to go.

At the end of the day, Mary found Nate in the Community Room making notations on his various charts and graphs.

"May I join you?" She asked as she entered the room.

"Come in, please. You seem to be the only one who wants to be anywhere near me. The rest of the crew freezes up as soon as I enter the room. Even my brothers escaped early. Did you know that Joe even called me BIG BROTHER and threatened to…"

"Yes, I know." She said, chuckling. "He'll get over it. He always does."

"It really is not funny," Nate complained. "I spent all of last week meeting with suppliers, organizing systems, and working through these flow charts and improvements. If they all would just pay attention to the details, things would be that much better around here. It's not my fault that things need to be more efficient. It's not like I changed everything the way my brothers did. I gave them their old menu back. I asked them for suggestions. I even worked out ways to make their jobs easier. Did they thank me? No way! Here I am, trying to help to make things better, and they treat me like I have the plague!"

Mary waited patiently until he was finished. "What did you learn today?" she asked.

"That they really don't like me," he answered, with a grimace. "There was even one card in my Suggestion box that read and I quote, 'stop messing with things and give us our bakery back!'"

Mary listened as Nate continued, listing for her the improvements he had discovered by his day of observation. As he went on, she showed appreciation for his findings, making little comments such as, "I never noticed that," or

"That would be easier." After about an hour she saw that he was winding down.

"So, it has been a long day. Are you almost ready to go?"

"I will be in a minute; I just want to gather up all my materials. Otherwise, the guys will throw them in the mop closet with Cardboard Allan. Did you know I found him in there this morning, propping up the buckets? There were a few times today when I thought Joe was going to lock ME in there, too."

"Let me help you," Mary said with a chuckle as she began to neatly stack the poster boards on the table. "Then we can lock up together."

And that is what they did. Mary helped Nate carry his materials to his car, and then he walked her to hers.

"I made a mess today, didn't I, Mary," he said as he held the car door and watched her fasten her seat belt.

"No, not a mess. Your way is just different and you missed a few key data points that you might have paid attention to, like anticipating how people would react to a level of structure that is natural to you but might be too much for them. But that's OK. They're adaptable and they'll recover.

However, you might want to stay out of Joe's kitchen for a few more days – just in case." She gave him a wink.

"Thanks Mary," Nate said with a wry smile as he closed her door. She put the car in drive and moved on down the street. From her rearview mirror, she could see him standing there watching. When she got to the stop sign at the corner, she looked back to see he was still there, just staring out into the night. But, then, she was not really surprised.

She'd expected him to be there, thinking things through.

### Little Spoonfuls

For more on structure and control,
see the Little Spoonfuls Appendix

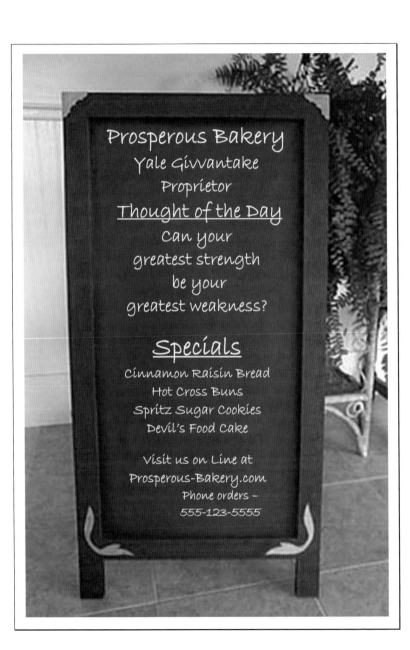

# Chapter 9 - Thursday

As Yale turned the key in the lock of *Prosperous Bakery* that Thursday morning, he was a bit concerned.

He'd spent the last week researching how to run bakeries and reading books on small family-run businesses. Then he had watched his older brothers each take their turn. While they had done some things right with their big ideas, maybe there were other things that would have worked better if they had spent more time thinking it through or done it a bit differently.

Now he was in the hot seat, but he just did not feel ready. He needed more information and he had run out of time!

He could hear Joe and the crew working in the kitchen and went back to let them know he had arrived.

The kitchen always had been his favorite part of the bakery. Everything was in its place and Joe rarely had to even look when he would reach out to find the next ingredient to add to the mix. The big book of Mom and Pop's recipes sat on a counter just in case anyone needed to reference it, and the list for supplies was posted on the bulletin board so that when something ran low, it could be added to the list.

*The Recipe: A Fable for Leaders and Teams*

"Morning," Joe said as he slid a tray of croissants into the big commercial oven and turned back to grab the next one. "All ready for your big day?"

"Yeah…maybe," Yale answered as he watched Joe slide another tray in place. "I want to try to get things back on a more even keel today, Joe. Is there anything you need from me today that I need to know about?"

"Not much, we can handle it here – but I will need your approval on the supply orders later today. With all the changes going on, we need to restock and order new items by 3:00 if we want them delivered in time for the weekend."

"Anything else?"

"Yeah, if you want things to run smoothly … keep your brothers out of my kitchen!"

"Got it," Yale said as he made his way back to the public area of *Prosperous Bakery*. There he found Mary and the rest of the crew preparing for opening.

"There you are," Mary said as she stood behind the counter. "Do you want me to call the team together for you?"

"Do we need a meeting? Yeah, maybe we do. Give me a minute to get my thoughts together and I will meet you all here by the counter for something quick." He moved over to the Welcome Station to gather his thoughts. Looking up at the signs and pictures on the wall, he reached for Ivan's sign and took it down. The suggestion box could stay -- that was a good idea, and maybe he'd keep it. Later in the day he would look at the suggestions that had already come in. He was pretty sure Mary had said she had put them on the desk in the back office.

The crew was assembled up front so he headed over to give them a few instructions before the doors officially opened. The little bells jingled over the door and he saw his brothers come in and take a seat at the back café table as he made his way to the counter

As he walked up to stand beside Mary, he began to speak to the team. "Our goal today is to get things back to business as usual. No big changes. I've been watching and the customers seem a bit confused. Keep the menu the same as it was yesterday, manage your workflow the way you have in the past…"

At that Suzie from the front counter raised her hand. "We actually did find some things that worked better yesterday, can we do them?"

"Yeah, maybe… that would be OK," Yale replied. "You all know your jobs. I trust you to do them. Just let me know if you need anything.

"Do you want to keep the pie pieces smaller?" asked Janey, the head waitress in the café.

"What did the customers say yesterday about the pie?"

"Mayor Maloney wanted to know who got the rest of his slice," someone answered.

"Yeah, maybe we should not have changed that – go back to the old way for now, and then I can let you know later on what we do long term. Anything else? Great! Let's get those doors open."

As the day went on, things were running pretty smoothly. With things back to business as usual, the line at the counter was manageable, and the café was back to normal, with customers lingering to read and chat.

Not bad, Yale thought to himself. I can do this pretty well if I don't say so myself. I hope the guys are taking notes. Sometimes the old ways are best after all.

Mary could see that Yale was pretty proud of himself, and things were going smoothly on the surface. But she had a few concerns. Throughout the day, the crew had gone to Yale with the usual little things that always came up. "Can we book this party so close to that one in the Community Room?" "Is it time to mark down the morning stock so we can move it?" "Business is picking back up. Do we need to change the re-order quantities?" And with every question the response went the same way. "Yeah…maybe… let me look into that… I'll get back to you." So simple, yet important, decisions were not getting made.

The lunch rush was over and Yale was back in the office with Joe. Mary had left them alone. Joe had always had a special relationship with Yale ever since he was boy. Then she heard Joe's voice loud and clear.

"For Pete's sake, man. Make a decision! If you don't, we won't have food to serve by Saturday. That order was due to the supplier 15 minutes ago. Make up your mind!" Joe stomped out of the office and towards the kitchen as Mary headed his way. "Do something!" he said to her as he pushed his way back through the swinging door.

Mary hurried back to the office, and there was Yale with his head in his hands. He looked up as she entered. "I meant to get the order in – really, I did. But there were questions about quantities and Joe was busy with the lunch rush, and then another salesman called today and said they might be cheaper and…"

Mary sat down beside him and tried to keep her cool. "It's OK. Take a deep breath. Let's just look at the list – our normal supplier will do for now and they'll stay open until we can call this in to them. Let's run down the order right now so you can call it in."

As they did, she began to see Yale's dilemma.

Today's order had to take them through the weekend and Saturday was Oliver's day. He had been marketing a special event at the bakery for the weekend and Yale could not decide whose numbers were right. Did he order to Joe's list or his brother's that doubled the usual levels? Mary helped him make the decision, based on her experience. "Double the order – there is nothing on here that we can't use later in the week if we end up with too much. This is the number one priority, so call it in now." After he had done so she asked, "What else do you have? "

As Yale went down the list of all of the decisions that he needed to get back to someone on, Mary walked him through the process, one by one, and they decided together. Then, she got up from the desk. "OK, you have a bunch of follow up calls to make. I'll let you get to it. If you need me, I'll be out front. "

Two hours later, the kitchen crew was gone for the day and the last of the café and counter team had closed up and

headed out. She and Yale were the only ones left at
*Prosperous Bakery*.

Just as she was walking back to check on him, he came out
of the office.

"Would you like to sit with me for a minute," she asked?

"Thanks," he said, taking a seat "And not just for waiting for
me to close up. Thanks for helping me before back in the
office."

"You're welcome. What did you learn from your day
today?"

"Maybe I learned that I'm not much of a leader or a decision
maker.

"Why do you say that?" she asked.

"You saw me. I was paralyzed and so was the team as they
waited for me to decide. These were not BIG decisions, just
lots of small ones, but I did not have all the information I
needed and I just got stuck. I wanted to ask the guys for
help, but I did not know how. They all had stood on their
own and here I was drowning. I just did not know how to
ask. I read about this in an article once. It brought me to a

dead stop.  What kind of leader can't even make a simple decision by himself?" Yale hung his head.

"Actually," said Mary, "Often it is a very good leader.  Some people need feedback before making a decision – it helps them to weigh options and then make the best call. "

"Like we did back in the office today when you helped me through the decision list?"

"Exactly.  Leaders like you need a team around them to exchange ideas and explore options.  Once they do, not only do they have a decision, they often have support for the decision from others too.  This is one of your greatest strengths.  Just don't let it bog you down.  It's smart to get someone to help you through it or to delegate it to someone who knows the positives and the negatives, and then to trust them to do it."

Mary patted Yale's hand, and then continued. "Keep in mind that there all kinds of ways of being a leader.  Each one is different.  Great leaders succeed based on the combined strengths of the skills of the people they gather around them to help them make decisions and get things done. By letting each step forward when their skill was most needed, they could accomplish more."

"How did you get to be so wise, Mary?" Yale asked.

"I'm not sure it's wisdom. Just experience. I've been at this a long time, and I had great teachers in your Mom and Pop.

"Over the years, I've made my share of mistakes, as we all do. They taught me that it's smart to reach out to others but sometimes you also just have to go with your instincts. You need to take a step, move forward, and let the journey unfold.

"Don't let a fear of being wrong keep you from making decisions when you need to. I have found that if you can communicate your goals to others the rest can almost always be worked out.

"Nothing in life works out perfectly 100% of the time. You just take what does work and use it. The rest of the time, you adjust, and try again. If you choose not to decide, you risk nothing but you gain nothing, Even if half of your choice is wrong and part of it is right, you still end up holding what is right. You are still farther ahead.

"In most cases, a small decision, or even a big one, gone wrong can offer a good lesson. The key is to learn from each choice and only try to repeat the successful ones."

Yale gave her a weak smile. "Yeah … maybe. But it sure can be daunting when all those decisions pile up on you."

"Yes, it can. But you did just fine and tomorrow those decisions will fall on Sam's shoulders, not yours. Tomorrow is his day. Well, are you about ready to go?"

"Absolutely, I'll walk you to your car."

He got the lights, while Mary waited at the door.

Together as they walked out the door to the jingling of bells, Yale thought with relief that the only decision he had left for the evening was what to have for dinner.

### Little Spoonfuls

Making decisions or delegating them is often the leader's job. When you don't have the answers, neither does your team.

See the Little Spoonfuls Appendix for insights into decision making.

# Chapter 10 – Friday

Friday was the day that Sam had been waiting for. He was excited about holding his first employee meeting and pleased to have the opportunity to share thoughts and ideas with the employees. He had asked everyone to come a little early so that everyone would have a chance to say their piece. Being the youngest, he knew how frustrating it could be when you felt like no one was listening to you, or you were left out of the conversation.

Ever since Ivan had started the suggestion box, Sam had been monitoring it. He'd reviewed all the ideas and suggestions. He also had ideas of his own but he wanted to hear from everyone else too. He had borrowed an easel and flip chart from his brother so that he could capture everyone's ideas to look at later. Now he was just waiting for everyone to arrive. For once, his brothers arrived first and took their place at the back café table. Then Mary came in and went back in to the kitchen to get Joe and the Kitchen Crew who had planned their schedule so that nothing was in the oven that would need to be tended during the meeting. He had even invited the afternoon crew to come in early so that everyone could participate together.

When they were all assembled, he started things off. "First, I have something to say to you all. … thank you. There is no place like *Prosperous Bakery*, and its magic comes from each of you. It is YOUR efforts, YOUR ideas and YOUR abilities that make this the place where people come to gather, to meet, and to find that special treat. YOU are what is special about *Prosperous Bakery* and it is you who worked side by side with our grandparents to make *Prosperous Bakery* what it is today," he said, pointing to the picture that hung over the Welcome Station.

"My brothers and I thank you for all that you've done, for all that you do, and for all that in the future we will do together." As he paused, everyone stood and applauded. The boy has a way with words, thought Mary.

"Now, as the next generation of Givvantakes takes *Prosperous Bakery* to new levels, we need your help. I'm not here to tell you where *Prosperous Bakery* is going. I am here to ask you. I've been reading cards from the suggestion box and watching and listening since I've been back. Now I am asking you to share your ideas. Mary, would you mind coming up here and capturing them for us so we don't miss any?"

Mary started to capture the ideas as Sam continued to hold his mini town hall with the staff. But as it continued, she started to wonder. Was he setting expectations too high? There was no way that he could implement all of these things on his own.

As the clock ticked on, it soon became time to wrap things up and open up *Prosperous Bakery* for the day. Sam thanked the team again and then went back to join his brothers in the café.

"So, Mr. President," asked Allan, "Just how do you plan to keep those campaign promises?"

"Yeah," added Yale, "Maybe you should have talked to us about this before you got the team all worked up."

Sam was taken aback. "What do you mean? I made it clear to the team that I was speaking on behalf of all of us. I did not promise to do it all alone – I couldn't – I can't."

"Are you sure?" asked Ivan. "From where I was sitting it sounded more like promises to me, and it may have to them, too. How do you think they'll react if no one acts on their so-called good ideas?"

Sam tried not to show his disappointed with his brothers' reactions. Yes, he knew they often did not listen to him, but he had been so sure that when the employees spoke up they would pay attention. He looked around the table at his brothers' closed expressions. Then he got up from his chair. "If you'll excuse me," he said to the group, "I need to check in with Joe and see how things are going in the kitchen."

"Think we might have been too hard on him?" Ivan asked as Sam walked towards the kitchen door. The brothers looked at each other for a moment.

"Nah" they chorused in unison.

Mary had been watching the group in the corner and had caught some of the exchanges between the brothers, especially the tail end. She was disappointed in all of them. This would bear some watching. She knew all too well that although Sam could put on a good front, underneath he could be easily hurt.

All through the day, as Sam moved from crew to crew, the response was the same. People were patting him on the back, sharing new ideas with him, and asking his opinion. But while he should have been standing tall, it appeared to Mary that the burden on his young shoulders was growing heavier and heavier. She wondered if Sam were beginning to realize that although he was getting people to contribute lots of great new ideas, some of those suggestions might be very hard to put into action, while others could be impossible without a lot of work and support from everyone.

Finally, the day was over and the crews were gone. Only Mary and Sam remained behind in *Prosperous Bakery*.

Mary went back into the office and brought out the roll of easel pages from the morning's presentation and walked over to where Sam sat at the corner café table where his brothers could normally be found. "What would you like me to do with these lists of suggestions you developed with the team this morning?" she asked.

"Oh, Mary, you are still here," Sam said, looking up. "I just don't know. At the time, I thought that it was such a great idea to ask the employees to get involved…but my brothers…"

"Hard on you, were they?" Mary asked.

"You could say that. It was pretty obvious that they don't see me as the true leader of *Prosperous Bakery*. I was just a stand-in-for-a-day to them. What will I tell the crew when nothing happens?"

"Do you believe these are good ideas," asked Mary as she handed him the rolled up pages.

"Some of them are great," Sam answered, "But how can I make them happen if I'm not accepted by my brothers as the leader? Everyone will be disappointed and it will all be my fault."

"I think you are confused here, Sam," said Mary. "Leadership is not about title or position. A leader is defined by his or her actions. It is your actions that demonstrates leadership and creates results – that's what earns you respect. You are an equal owner with your brothers in *Prosperous Bakery*. You have a voice and the opportunity to be *a leader* whether you are chosen to be **the** *leader*, or not.

"Keep in mind that there are many ways to lead, and all kinds of leaders. Finding the style that works best for you isn't always easy. But once you do, others will recognize it and be more willing to follow your lead. You must first see yourself as a leader before anyone else can. It's all up to you and how you choose to use your voice. You did great today. Don't give up now. You're just getting started."

Sam took the rolled up papers and stood up. "You're right. I can choose to be *a leader* no matter what happens. Thanks, Mary."

"You're welcome. Any time" Mary replied. "But, for now, this loyal follower has had a long day. It's time to head for home. Want to lead the way?"

So together, Mary and Sam went through the final closing list for *Prosperous Bakery* that had been developed by Yale for the crew. They checked the kitchen and behind the counter to ensure that everything was turned off for the night.

Again Mary stood by the door as the youngest one of what she always thought of as her boys went to turn off the lights. Then Sam opened the door to a jingling of bells and they headed into the night.

"Can I walk you to your car, Mary?"

"Thank you, Sam" she answered. "Lead on."

### Little Spoonfuls

Communication is a key leadership skill. Often leaders communicate through promises. But equally important is how you keep them.

See the Little Spoonfuls Appendix for insights into team communication.

# Chapter 11 – Saturday

Oliver was always entertaining, no matter what he did.  His brothers were looking forward to an exciting Saturday.   No matter what happened it was guaranteed to be fun!

It had been a tough week at *Prosperous Bakery* and the crowd had started to taper off as each brother had his day.  All the changes were just too much for some of the regulars, but they had seen the posters around town advertising the *Prosperous Bakery* Saturday Celebration.  Oliver was a town favorite and sure to draw a crowd.

Mary and the guys all pulled into the back lot by the service entrance at the same time.  They could not park across the street as they normally did. The lot was FULL and a line had formed outside the doors and down the block.

Entering though the back kitchen door, they were greeted by pandemonium.  Joe will be in a real tizzy this time, Mary thought to herself.

And so he was.  "Mary, l thank God you are here.  Did you see that line?  There is no way we can be ready for all those people.  Did you see that crowd?  I wouldn't have believed it – and I certainly did not order for it!"

*The Recipe: A Fable for Leaders and Teams*

"I did," said Yale, "the extra supplies are in the store room."

Mary tuned to point a finger at the Givvantake brothers. "Stay right here," she said as she hurried over to the door from the kitchen to the café.

As she swung though the door, she saw Oliver there in all his glory, surrounded by small buckets of confetti. There were flashing lights, the blare of live music, and costumed characters, one dressed as a sprinkled cupcake and another as a carrot cake muffin, skipping out the door to mingle with the waiting crowd.

"Oliver," Mary called out over the music. "I need you in the kitchen please, NOW."

As they came back into the kitchen, Mary turned to Joe and said, "Help me up on that stool."

"OK, folks, Listen up! Oliver, you have created a wonderful opportunity – but if we don't get some teamwork, and fast, it could turn into a disaster. The team was not ready for this kind of a crowd. So here is what we need to do…

"Joe, modify the menu quickly so we can push as much quantity through the ovens as they can handle.

"Yale, go get some of the guys from the wait staff and move the extra supplies into the kitchen so Joe has what he needs. And then stick around to help him so the wait staff can get back in front again to help there.

"Ivan and Nate, you've spent the most time with the counter and café staff. Go out there to help the crew. They're going to need extra hands.

"Allan and Sam, you've got crowd control. Work the line, give them samples, be charming – you know what to do.

"Oliver, you are with me. We need to call Mayor Maloney and get some police on the street to handle that crowd."

"Uh, Mary," Oliver said. "I don't think we'll need to call the mayor. He and Chief Donavan are at the head of the line, with their grandkids."

"Well, what are we waiting for? Let's get them.

"Remember everyone – teamwork!" she called out as she and Oliver hurried toward the front doors.

For Mary, the rest of the day passed in a blur. There was no lull between breakfast and lunch. The crowds kept getting bigger all day as word spread about the party going on at *Prosperous Bakery*. Chief Donovan finally called in some officers to close off the block for safety's sake and the party spilled out into the street. Joe kept the ovens going with the simplest items to mass produce cookies, cupcakes and other small snacks. Thank goodness the bakery did not have any wedding cakes to deliver today, he thought.

Everyone on the team did their part, and they managed to pull it all off, just barely, as the band played gaily throughout the morning and afternoon while the costumed sprinkled cupcake and the carrot cake muffin danced with patrons on the sidewalk out front. It was amazing to see what they could do when each of the brothers focused his energies on doing what he did best. Mary had never been prouder of them.

At 5:00, an hour before closing, the band announced the last song of the afternoon. As the music tapered off, so did the crowds, and the crew began to clean up the confetti and other party paraphernalia that was all around.

"Whew!" was all anyone could say.

It had been an awesome exciting day but it was clear everyone had tapped deeply into their energy supply, thought Mary. They would need some time to recharge. They were starting to drag a bit and tonight's conversation would be important. Fun and excitement is all well and good, but no one can run at full speed for too long.

*Prosperous Bakery's* cupboards were almost bare. There was not a crumb left behind. They might have been exhausted, yet just as they had all day, each of the brothers pitched in to help set things to rights. By 6:15, the doors were closed and *Prosperous Bakery* was almost back to normal again.

"Gentlemen," Mary called from the kitchen doorway, "I'm heading over to my cottage, please close up. I'll see you at eight."

And without a backwards glance, she slipped out through the kitchen and into her car.

As she drove home, she marveled at how a potential disaster became a success, not just for *Prosperous Bakery,* but for the *Givvantake Team* as she was beginning to think of the brothers.

# Chapter 12 –Saturday Night

That night, promptly at 8:00, another set of little bells jingled at Mary's cottage. The bells were just like the ones at *Prosperous Bakery*. The Givvantakes had given them to her as a housewarming present when she moved into the cottage many years ago. Mary loved her bells. Each time she heard them, she again felt Mom and Pop's love and support around her.

When she opened the door, there they stood… the *Givvantake Team,* Allan, Ivan, Yale, Nate, Sam, and Oliver, who was holding a big bouquet of red roses.

"We would have brought coffee and cookies," said Allan with a chuckle, "But after today's event there is not a drop to be had or a crumb left over. We even sold the box set aside for tonight!"

Everyone laughed. It felt great to celebrate the day's accomplishments, even if at this moment there was not a cookie to be found anywhere in *Prosperous Bakery*. It had been a long day and while earlier they had been exhausted, by now had all caught their second wind. The day's near disaster and great success had them all wired.

They would not want to run at that pace every day, thought Mary, but to see the team in action like today….it was wonderful. This is the tradition and the legacy the Givvantakes left behind.

"I was proud of you all today," said Mary as they gathered around her big kitchen table. "I've asked most of you this separately, but never as a group. What did you learn this week?"

Allan started them off. "I learned that having great ideas is not enough. Too much change, too fast, and without the right plan to back it up can lead to disappointing results. An idea is only as good as its execution. It's not all about me. It's all about us."

"So true, Allan" said Mary. "It's never all about me for a leader." Mary got up from the table and walked over to the counter to pick up a whisk and hand it to Allan. "The right amount of change is wonderful to stir things up, just as this whisk can take simple eggs and whip them into a fine froth. The trick is to not agitate things too long. Otherwise the batter gets tough. This whisk was one of Mom's favorites. I want you to keep it as my gift to you."

"On Tuesday I learned that the grass is not always greener on the other side of the fence," added Ivan. "I always wanted to have Allan's place at the front of the line, but once I got there I found that I am much stronger and more valuable behind the scenes than I am front and center. And frankly, I like it better behind the scenes too."

"Excellent, Ivan," Mary replied, as she went to the cupboard and pulled out one of her own well-seasoned baking sheets and placed it on the table before him. "Knowing who you are, and what you are best at, provides a steadiness and stability to your team that acts as a platform of support, just as a cookie sheet does to the most delicate of pastries as they bake in the oven."

"I've always focused on the details," added Nate. "I pay attention to the little things so it's not my fault when things fall through the cracks or get overlooked. But I learned that too much emphasis on data and little things can get you bogged down and create tension and feelings of uneasiness. Too much efficiency can backfire. And in my case, it even can be life-threatening. I think Joe wanted to murder me!"

"Only for a little while," Mary said with a smile, as she moved to a drawer and selected a set of nested tin measuring cups that were so old that the name of the company that once made them was long worn away but the engraved marker lines were still strong and clear. "Your strength brings a precision and measurement to the team just as the measuring cups allow for exact precision each time they are used. Baking is an art where precision is needed and this is where you excel."

"Yeah, and maybe you can help me on the decision side," Yale said, with a chuckle. "For me, it was all about decisions. I've always thought that seeing both sides of any question was my greatest strength. But when lots of decisions needed to be made quickly – it was just too much. If Mary had not stepped in and walked me through the orders last week, we would not have had anything to serve to the crowd today."

Mary pointed to a small antique scale on the counter. "This, Yale, is my gift to you. Like the scale, your gift to the team is that you weigh the options by making sure both sides are balanced. Out of all of your brothers, you are the most likely to look carefully at opportunities and then your brothers can support you with their weight, too."

"My turn … I have something to say," said Sam, as his brothers groaned. "No, really you guys – listen up. As the youngest, I listen a lot  and then can speak up for others."

"You are a lot like your grandmother in that way, Sam," said Mary, pulling a small notebook out of her apron pocket and setting it before him.

"Mom's recipe book still sits on the counter in the *Prosperous Bakery* kitchen, filled not just with her favorite recipes but also with many notes as to the comments and suggestions customers had made through the years. It was those notes that allowed her to perfect her recipes. This notebook can be your start, a place to keep the ideas you gather so you can put them into action. Pop gave Mom a box of these little notebooks every year at Christmas for her notes so that she could keep them close and share with us what she observed and the invaluable lessons she learned."

"Thank you, Mary" Sam said. "As part of this family, I have a voice people listen and respond to. We got some great suggestions from the crew and customers yesterday. Some have a ways to go, but if we work on them together *Prosperous Bakery* can be even better than it is now."

"And *Prosperous Bakery* is already GREAT!" Oliver exclaimed, throwing out his arms. "I know you guys think my ideas are sometimes a bit over the top, but did you see those crowds today? The customers loved us. The place was packed. And thanks to all of you pitching in and helping out, people will be talking about today for a REALLY long time. Just imagine what it's going to do for business!"

"Oliver, your gift is to always provide the icing on the cake," Mary said as she handed him a mixing bowl filled with decorating tubes and tips. "As the team's creative mind you bring excitement and ideas that highlight what is best about *Prosperous Bakery*, just as these tools add beauty and color to the cakes and cookies that graced the bakery's shelves. You just need to remember not to overdo it."

"I know, I know," Oliver replied, looking at Mary and his brothers, "We might not be able to take things over the top every day, but if we do it on selected days…just imagine," he said with a grin.

"That's quite a list," said Mary as she looked around the table. "But this week was supposed to be about helping you all decide who the best person to lead *Prosperous Bakery* will be, now that you own it together. Have you found the answer to that question?"

"Yeah, maybe," said Yale. "We talked about it while we were cleaning up after the celebration today. What we started to realize is that we make a pretty good team."

"I've been looking at the details and tracking our results over the week," added Nate. "Individually we each had some wins – and OK – our share of challenges too…"

"It's not all about me, or Ivan… or any of us," added Allan. "What made the biggest impact was when we worked off of each other's strengths today. Then things really came together."

"So on behalf of my brothers, what we're trying to say…" said Sam, "is that we want another week to try to run *Prosperous Bakery* as a team with each of us contributing what we do best."

"We still have some details to work out," Yale added. "But we think this might be the right plan for *Prosperous Bakery.*"

Mary was amazed, and so very proud of them. As the conversation continued well into the night they were making plans and sharing ideas. Each had a piece to contribute and while they did not always agree, or reach decisions quietly – they were blending together like the finest of ingredients.

Each of them is unique, thought *Mary.* They are starting to see that what they each bring a unique toolset to the team and that when they use them together they can get the job done.

Mom and Pop knew that, and so did I. Now they are learning it too.

Sam sat listening to his brothers and adding in his thoughts, plus the ideas that had come from his Friday team meeting. But he was also watching Mary. He could tell she was fading at last. After all, she was a lot older that they were.

"Mary," he said. "We'll clean up here. You should call it a day."

"Are you sure?" she asked, looking around the table. "We're sure," they replied. "And, Mary," added Ivan, "Sleep in tomorrow, you need your rest. You haven't had a day off in a week. You must be exhausted."

So as Mary made her way to her bedroom in the back of her cottage, the *Givvantake Team* cleaned up her kitchen.

They put everything in its place, just as she always did, then together opened the cottage door to the jingling of bells and made their way home for the night.

Back in the bedroom, Mary smiled. As quiet as they had tried to be, the cottage was small and she had lain there listening in the dark from her room in the back as the brothers had put her kitchen to rights.

"Oh, Mom and Pop," she whispered. "What a wonderful team they are becoming.. I hope you can see them."

### Little Spoonfuls

The best lessons are the ones learned through experience.

See the Little Spoonfuls Appendix for some hints on creating learning experiences for your team.

# Chapter 13 – Another week

Sunday morning the *Givvantake Team* was back at *Prosperous Bakery* bright and early. They even beat Joe and the kitchen crew in for the first time ever.

Sam led the team meeting, with all his brothers standing behind him. Since he always had something to say, they decided this time they'd let him say it.

They've bonded, thought Mary, and it shows. They are using their strengths and relying on each other and the greater team for what they need.

'They even look more confident and united," she whispered to Joe.

Together the Givvantakes divided up their responsibilities, with Allan and Sam taking turns manning the busy Welcome Station since they thrived in the fast-changing environment, talking with customers, and making everyone feel welcome.

Ivan and Yale worked the back office, deciding what needed to be quickly reordered since they had run through so many of the supplies on Saturday.

Oliver parked himself in the Community Room with his laptop to work on the next marketing campaign. Nate sat beside him with his own laptop to work up a revised operating plan.

When Mary arrived around noon, *Prosperous Bakery* was full of old friends. She went from table to table saying hello, chatting about yesterday's exciting event, stopping to share a cup of tea, or checking in with the counter crew.

Each brother was striving to do what he did best. It was not that one talent was better than the other, or that any role was more important. As Mom Givvantake used to say, "Everybody equally matters." Things were going so well, she did not need to stay out front for long. Instead she went back into the kitchen to visit with Joe.

Monday morning, the brothers held their first official team meeting, reviewing plans, discussing the list of changes that Allan and Sam had pulled together, and prioritizing which ones they would tackle first, and how they could, as a team, best implement them. It was great to see some of the new ideas and products incorporated with the longstanding customer favorites. The *Prosperous Bakery* crew and the next generation were finding their rhythm together.

"They are truly becoming a team at last," thought Mary.

The first change they implemented was a new rule –

> *Every team member at* **Prosperous Bakery** *is a key ingredient and important to the team.*
>
> *So that everyone can be at their best, each team member will have TWO scheduled days off each week.*

The *Givvantakes* also decided that Mary, as the longest standing employee of *Prosperous Bakery,* should choose her two days first. She chose Thursday and Friday.

As the week progressed, Mary marveled at how well the ingredients were starting to blend together. Each ingredient stood beautifully on its own, while also complimenting the others to create a far greater flavor.

Small improvements were being implemented with feedback from customers and the *Prosperous Bakery* crew, and, most importantly, the brothers began to not only see each other in a new light, they treated each other with the same care as they would a freshly baked cookie being moved from the tray to the cooling rack.

Wednesday night after closing, Mary met in the Community Room with the *Givvantake Team* since Thursday and Friday would be her days off.

"Are you sure you don't need me?" she asked, as they assembled at the big oak table.

"We have it under control, Mary, enjoy your days off," Allan told her.

"Just remember, the unveiling ceremony for the new sign is Saturday at 8 AM," said Oliver. "I promise – nothing over the top, but we don't want you to miss it. Mayor Maloney and the Chief will be here with the folks from the paper and the Chamber of Commerce. "

"Yeah, maybe, even Mrs. Birdwell and the Garden Club ladies will come in early for it. And you would not want to miss them." Yale said with a smile.

"Well, good. Whose turn is it to close up tonight?" she asked.

"That would be us," answered Nate and Sam.

"I'll say good night, then," she said, gathering up her sweater and purse.

"Wait up," said Yale. "I'll walk you to your car."

After the brothers heard the little bells jingle over the front door, Nate turned to Oliver. "Is everything ready for Saturday?"

"It will be," Oliver answered. "I spoke to the sign company today and they promised to deliver it, hang it, and drape it on Friday so that it can be officially unveiled Saturday morning."

"Great. Now that it's safe for me to go back into the kitchen again, thanks to Yale putting in a good word for me, I spoke with Joe. The cake will be ready and in the Community Room for after the ceremony. We just have to keep her out of here that morning so it does not spoil the surprise," added Nate.

"OK ! It sounds like we're set," said Allan, and with that he too headed for home, leaving his brothers to close up.

### Little Spoonfuls

Pulling together a championship team is a key leadership skill. See the Little Spoonfuls Appendix for some secret ingredients for better team formation.

# Chapter 14 - The Unveiling

When Mary arrived Saturday morning, there was again a crowd in front of *Prosperous Bakery*. There was no music or dancing baked goods this time around, just a group of regular customers including Mayor Maloney, Chief Donavan, Janet from the Chamber with a photographer from the local paper, and Mrs. Birdwell with the ladies from the Garden Club. Standing with them were all six of the Givvantake brothers and every single member of the *Prosperous Bakery* crew.

"Oh, my," said Mary. "Am I late? I thought you said 8:00. Don't tell me I am the last one here."

"No, Mary," said Mayor Maloney. "We all arrived a bit early. But now that everyone is here, shall we begin?"

With that the photographer moved into position, and the brothers split up three to a side, to place their hands on the ropes attached to the canvas drape that covered the new sign for *Prosperous Bakery*. As the crowd gaily chanted, "One – Two – Three" they gave a tug and down came the canvas amid cheers and applause.

The sign was beautiful. In big gold letters it read:

```
┌─────────────────────────────────────────┐
│                                           │
│           Prosperous Bakery               │
│                                           │
│     A Givvantake Brothers Enterprise      │
│                                           │
│        Mary Keeper, Proprietor            │
│                                           │
│                                           │
└─────────────────────────────────────────┘
```

Mary's hands flew to her mouth in surprise. She had not had a clue as to what the brothers had been up to.

"Hey, look," said Sam, pointing at Mary. "She's speechless."

Each of the brothers could not have wished for more.

As the brothers ushered the dignitaries and crowd inside, Joe came up to take Mary's arm. "Surprised you, did they?" he asked her. Mary just nodded. "Well, there's more. You might just need this," he added, pulling a fresh white handkerchief from the pocket of his spotlessly clean baker's apron.

Joe took Mary's arm and led her under the sign and through the door as the little bells jingled. Together they walked to the Community Room where on the table a beautiful cake that looked just like the Prosperous Bakery sign sat in a place of honor on the big oak table next to the picture of Mom and Pop Givvantake that had been taken last Christmas with the crew.

"Ladies and Gentlemen," said Sam. "Thank you for joining us today for the unveiling of our new sign and to congratulate our new leader, Mary Keeper." Sam paused to let the crowd applaud.

"Mary has been at the heart of *Prosperous Bakery*, for as long as we all can remember. She was Mom and Pop's right hand and a trusted friend to them, just as she has been a friend and guide not only to our *Prosperous Bakery* team, but to so many more in our community. I know you love her just as we do. Let's give her one more round of applause."

Mary looked around the room at the Givvantake Team, and all of *Prosperous Bakery's* many friends.

"Speech, speech" called Oliver as he led Mary to a place of honor in front of the cake, and the cameras flashed again. "Thank you," she said, gazing around the room. "Thank you all…"

The room was filled with people and good conversation and the air was perfumed with the wonderful scents of fresh coffee and *Prosperous Bakery's* wares.

You could feel the joy, and Mary hoped that Mom and Pop, wherever they were, could feel it, too.

As the team posed together along the wall for a new photo, Mary stood in the center holding the photo of Mom and Pop. She was surrounded by the Givvantake brothers and the crew.

It was a great picture and it would grace the Welcome Station at *Prosperous Bakery* for many years to come.

### Little Spoonfuls

Nothing is more powerful than acknowledging a job well done.

See the Little Spoonfuls Appendix for insights into the power of acknowledgements and rewards.

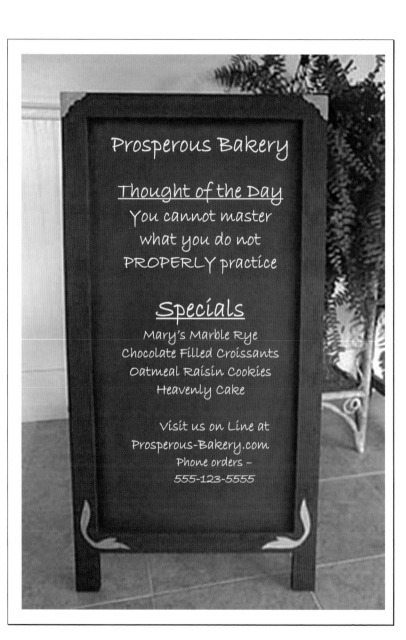

# Epilogue – The Recipe

That Saturday, after the celebration was over, Mary and the Givvantake brothers again gathered around the big oak table in the Community Room.

Joe and the kitchen crew had packaged up the rest of the cake, and the café crew had cleaned things up out front.

Mary had asked the brothers to stay with her. Now that the crowds were gone, there was just one last thing to do.

From her purse she removed six envelopes.

Each one had the name of one of Mom and Pop's grandsons written on the front.

"I've been wondering," she began, looking around the table, "why none of you ever have asked me about *The Recipe*. It was part of the gift your grandparents left to you, and I have been keeping it safe. But you never asked about it. So now, at the end of what has been a perfect day, I thought this might be the right time to share it with you."

With that she handed each of them their envelope.

The room was quiet as each brother carefully opened his envelope. Inside was a copy of a letter that Mom and Pop had written to Mary.

Dear Mary,

When you read this, our time here with you will be done.

You have been far more than a friend to us over the years. You became part of our family. Together with you, we have formed the foundation of our beloved bakery. You have given us so much and we hope you will do one more thing for us.

*Prosperous Bakery* will pass down to our grandsons, as will *The Recipe* that has been the secret to *Prosperous Bakery's* success.

*The Recipe* is not for a cookie or a loaf of bread. It is the combination of the right ingredients, the right utensils and the easy-to-follow directions for building a winning business.

*The Recipe* is the one we practiced and perfected together with you over the years. And now, we are asking that you share it with our grandsons. Help them to keep it safe and to see its value. When they do, they will keep it close at hand and use it well. When they do, it will help guide them as they celebrate the good times and survive the more challenging ones.

Every good recipe has three components:

**The Ingredients**

Every good cookie needs the right ingredients to make a perfect batch.

A successful business and a rewarding life need the right mix of people and skills to make a perfect team. They are:

- Innovators
- Motivators
- Communicators
- Researchers
- Planners
- Implementers

**The Utensils**

The second component of every good cookie recipe is the list of utensils. As a baker, you need a bowl, a whisk, a spoon, measuring cups, cookie sheets and a cooling rack. These are the tools that help you get the job done.

The essential tools of a great team are its values. The values we have built together over the years include:

- Embracing others ideas
- Being willing to ask and be asked
- Trusting others and being worthy of trust
- Keeping our commitments
- Doing what it takes to be the best

**Directions**

The third component of a good cookie recipe is the directions. You need to measure, mix, stir and bake all at just the right time. The directions show you where to focus your energies.

A successful business needs a team that is willing to:
- Experiment
- Practice
- Affirm
- Believe

You cannot make a good cookie without all three parts of the recipe just as you also cannot have a successful business, a winning team, or a rewarding life without the right components.

With love, Mom and Pop

One by one, the brothers set down their copies of *The Recipe*.

"We never even asked about *The Recipe*," Oliver said quietly to himself.

"And, since we never asked, you decided to show us, didn't you, Mary?" Allan asked.

"It was not about showing you *The Recipe*. It was more about letting you discover it," she answered.

"We might read a lesson, or hear it from a teacher, but until we live it and experience it, it is easy to miss its true meaning.

"It is through doing that we truly discover what is really important.

"You each had the components of *The Recipe* all around you.

"Everything you needed was here in *Prosperous Bakery*.

"The little signs and pictures your grandparents posted on the walls and by the register.

"The culture they had built with our customers and crew was there to support you.

"And each of you brought a key ingredient with your own special talents." Mary paused and looked pointedly at each of the brothers.

"But with the loss of your grandparents and everything going on, you were distracted. You each needed to discover it for yourselves, in your own way, and in your own time." Mary took a sip of her coffee, and then continued. "I've just tried to be a guide along the discovery path so that you didn't get sidetracked along the way.

"You, Allan, are the team's innovator. Your talent for discovering and bringing fresh ideas to the team will allow us to always be different and a step ahead. We would not want our business or our team to get stale, and with you around that won't happen.

"Oliver, you are a great motivator. With your talents, our team is energized and moving forward. Just as Allan keeps us from getting stale, you have the power to move people in a direction and keep the ideas and actions flowing.

"Sam's strength is communication. Not only does he speak well, he listens. This allows people to feel heard and valued, while allowing information to be shared.

"Together, you all will always be able to count on Yale to research and plan every detail. With him as part of the team, you will know that you are standing on solid ground.

"Ivan's talent will help you all follow through on the plan. His role allows each of you to move more easily from step to step.

"Your grandparents and I knew that. Each of you brings unique talents and assets to *Prosperous Bakery* and more importantly to each other as a family."

"What our grandparents left us as *Prosperous Bakery's* values will guide us, connect us, and make us stronger as a whole," added Oliver.

"That's right" said Mary. "And if you ever need a reminder, you simply need to look at your recipe card. It's the same recipe that has kept the bakery, our crew and your grandparents together for half a century.

"There are pieces of *The Recipe* all around you. They are on the plaques on the wall, in the welcome sign on the door. In the photos where we embrace each other and in the traditions like Pop's old baker's table, the one Joe still uses today. It represents our traditions, and it has been around so long that each nick and scratch has its own story to tell. All over the over the bakery are sprinkles of The Recipe's wisdom.

"And as to the directions, you are already following them," she added. "Over the last few weeks I have watched you experiment with new ways of doing things. Each of you have put your unique talents into practice, measured your results and adapted where you needed to. You are well on your way to making *Prosperous Bakery* an even bigger success," Mary concluded.

"We succeed in all of this because you guided us, Mary," said Sam. "We might have figured out how to use *The Recipe* on our own, but you helped us get there faster."

"Yeah," said Yale, "And maybe we can make our own addition to *The Recipe*."

"We already did," shared Allan. "We added one of the most important ingredients of all. We chose a trusted and respected leader and added her to the mix."

"And she's a *Keeper*," Oliver added as they all laughed.

"Mary, there is one question you never really answered when I asked it before," Yale reminded her.

"Mom and Pop left us *Prosperous Bakery* and *The Recipe*. They called these gifts their treasures. You said that Mom and Pop shared their treasures with you long ago, but you never said what they were. Where you talking about *Prosperous Bakery* and *The Recipe*, too?

"No," said Mary. "My treasures are even more precious to me than a business or *The Recipe*.

The treasure that the Givvantakes shared with me was their family. They gave me all of you."

### Little Spoonfuls

Our greatest lessons are learned through experience.

See the Little Spoonfuls Appendix for insights into creating learning experiences for your teams.

# Little Spoonfuls

Tips and Exercises

For

Leaders and Teams.

# **TRUST**

The word TRUST is frequently misused or used so often that the importance and value of it is diminished.

Too often we see how trust can be shattered in many areas of our lives – from business to the home front. Yet without trust it is almost impossible for an individual, a leader or a team to successfully navigate change, overcome obstacles, or become resilient

Change takes many forms. It can appear as a new leader or member of a team, a new product, or a new way of doing things. Your company may be setting new goals, direction, or changes for itself or the environment around you may be driving change. In our home life we may face many changes, too, such as a new relationship, a new child, a new job, or a new neighborhood.

With change come natural fears or concerns. Change can make others feel insecure, or it can bring new challenges. Everybody feels vulnerable sometimes. Trust is the key element you need to overcome it. Yet you may also find that when change is all around you, a foundation of trust is difficult to build or maintain.

Trust does not just happen. It has to be earned, and earned repeatedly. Too often we confuse trust with acceptance, and they are not the same thing.

Trusting relationships are open to questions and challenges from the team. In fact, the raising of these questions and challenges is a good sign that your team trusts you enough to raise them.

Another mistake we make too often is to assume that once trust is earned, it stays in play. Trust often is hard to build and easy to lose. As leaders and teammates, it is KEY that we continue to demonstrate trustworthiness - - always!

Building trust is not a quick process. Even when someone is said to be trustworthy, human behavior often dictates that we need to test for ourselves.

Trust is built not on words, but through actions and evidence. When we do what we say we will, we build trust. When we do the opposite – we get the opposite - and the trust bond can be severely damaged.

The difference between a good leader and a great one is the ability to build solid trust relationships and to keep them strong. Once trust is earned, it is an invaluable asset that can make the difference between surviving tough times with challenges and obstacles, and achieving success.

The ability to develop trust is not a skill set or a strategy. It's a way of being.

### Keeper's Keys:

**Myth**: Once you gain trust it's never lost.
**Truth**: Trust needs to be earned repeatedly and demonstrated often.

**Myth**: Someone can pick and choose when he wants to be trusted.
**Truth**: Behaviors in one aspect of your life ALWAYS touch others. It cannot be turned on and off.

**Myth**: Once people are untrustworthy, they are always untrustworthy.
**Truth**: People can change. With experience, age, and wisdom, one can learn to be trustworthy.

**Myth**: Religion teaches trust.
**Truth**: Religion is based on faith. While trust and faith often go hand in hand, they are not the same thing. People learn and earn trust from different areas of their lives.

## Food for Thought:

1. What does trust mean to me?

2. What are the qualities I need to see in someone in order to trust them?

3. What types of evidence do I leave for others that show that I am trustworthy? (Think of real examples.)

4. Are there things about me or past experiences that prevent me from trusting others? Are these things that I want to overcome?

5. If I wanted to create a trusting relationship with someone else – what would I do first, second, and third? What would they need to do to earn trust with me?

# CONFLICT
# AND
# CONSENSUS

All great teams experience conflict from time to time, whether it's a partnership of two or a team of many. Conflict is a key component to a team's strength and to its longevity. It will come up. Expect it.

<u>A conflict and a fight are not the same thing</u>.

There is a clear distinction between conflict and fighting. Conflict is a challenge or push back on ideas, concepts, or knowledge. Here the focus is on facts and subjects. Fighting is more personal and can be emotionally connected and charged. Fighting polarizes people and can rock the foundation of your team when things get personal and become focused on someone's actions or feelings, especially around a position of right or wrong.

When we are young, conflict and fighting are often lumped together. As children we are told to play nicely and as teens often not to talk back. Instead we would be better off if we taught our children to recognize conflict from an early age, and demonstrated through our own actions how constructively to work through, react to and internalize conflict. Since most of us did not learn these skills, they need first to be relearned, and then practiced to change our connection, feelings and relationship with the word "conflict" itself, and the experience.

Constructive conflict is not built on a win or lose premise, but is a form of questioning to find a better answer or solution, to reach an overall feeling of satisfaction and contribution. Only through conflict resolution can we ever reach consensus, let alone achieve a positive outcome.

Conflict is not "bad".

When we discourage conflict, we encourage compliance. We've all seen the people who say "yes" to everything. They may be easy people to get along with, but they won't necessarily be your strongest contributors. While agreement is easier than conflict, the ones who question the status quo often provide the ingredient that acts as a catalyst to move you forward or equally importantly, supply the voice of reason to point out things you might have overlooked.

Without challenges and questions we do not learn – in both the contexts of business and life. Conflict gets us to look at our beliefs and positions in a new way. More importantly, it helps us determine what information might be misunderstood, incomplete, or no longer viable.

When conflict has passed, we may still be holding true to our position, but just maybe we will have learned something new about why you and fellow members fell to one side or another as part of the process.

Conflict often brings out new information that when it is applied becomes knowledge. And as the saying goes, knowledge is power, but only if you allow the process to unfold. The key to making good use of constructive conflict is for the leader not to abuse that power, showing respect for every person and their right to their opinion.

Working within boundaries, and with clear guidelines for reaching consensus, or better yet, agreement, will help your team and your organization. Developing a process, created and agreed upon by the team, on what is healthy and defines what is off limits, makes constructive conflict a productive process.

We've often been taught to find another's weak spot and use it to our advantage. As leaders, our job is to ensure that each member of the team is protected and defended against others who might want to take advantage of this vulnerability. The team can then moderate its members to

make sure the rules stay intact for the development of the
team and for a greater good.

## Keeper's Keys

**Myth**: Conflict is a bad thing
**Truth**: Conflict often breaks down barriers and makes way
for new growth, change and success.

**Myth**: Conflict and fighting is the same thing.
**Truth**: Conflict is subject based. Fighting is emotionally
based.

**Myth:** Conflict cannot be controlled.
**Truth**: Conflict becomes constructive when it stays within
agreed upon boundaries, guidelines, and rules that are put
into play and agreed upon by the team.

## Food for Thought:

1. What is the first memory I have of conflict? How does that affect how I view conflict today?

2. Does conflict make me feel uncomfortable?

3.  When facing a challenge, do I respond with logic or with emotion?

4.  What are three tools I can use to help move my team toward addressing conflict constructively?

5.  Conflict resolution most frequently ends in consensus.  Is consensus ALWAYS the right solution?

# <u>DEALING WITH CHANGE</u>

Change is a fact of life. Nothing stays the same forever.

As leaders and teams, sometimes we drive change and sometimes change drives us. But either way it is a given.

Change happens.

So recognizing that change will be the only constant, how can you make change work to your advantage?

In the story, we saw that when Allan introduced too much change, too soon and too fast, such change was not always a good thing. Change can take you in the opposite direction from where you are trying to go if you do not work through it well.

Whether we are initiating change or reacting to it will play a big part in our outcomes. Most people naturally are change resistant to one level or another. Even the most adventurous among us have a limit on just how much change we are

137
*The Recipe: A Fable for Leaders and Teams*

comfortable with.   We need time to regroup and replenish our personal resources. But here are some tried and true tips that can help you and your teams as you work through changes.

- Communicate consistently and often.
- Pay attention to body language and the unspoken messages they are sending you.
- Research all your options before deciding which direction to go.
- If you are initiating change, give clear instructions. Help the people affected by the change understand WHY the change will be made, and if possible, HOW the change will make the situation better.
- If the change is something outside of your direct control, fighting it is not the answer.  Instead do your best to understand how you can work it to your team's advantage and move forward.

*The Recipe: A Fable for Leaders and Teams*

**Keeper's Keys:**

**Myth:** Change can be managed.
**Truth:** Change happens. Sometime we control it and sometimes we cannot. In those times the best you can do is work through it and try to build the best possible solution. Change cannot be managed, but it can be anticipated.

**Myth:** Change is temporary.
**Truth:** Change is constant. As soon as you work through one change challenge, a new one will rise up to take its place.

**Myth:** People fear change.
**Truth:** Not all people fear change – but many do not like it. The best thing a leader can do is to address the unknown and bring clarity to the how and why of the change that is going to happen.

## Food for Thought:

1.   What is your strongest memory around change?

2.   Are you comfortable with initiating change?

3. How does change make you feel when it is initiated by others or brought on by outside factors beyond your control?

4. How can you help others work through change resistance or fear?

# AWARENESS

As we saw in the story about Ivan, often a level of self awareness can be vitally important to your individual or as a member of a team.

It affects how you view yourself and how others see you. Too often how we see ourselves may be different than how we truly are or are perceived to be by others.

It is often said that if you don't know where you are going, you will never get there. It is through self awareness that you find your purpose. When it comes to self awareness, if you are unclear on your innate talents, plus what you personally want and need to make the most of them, you will very rarely find it.

Luckily, there are many tools on the market that individuals and teams can use to help them better understand themselves, and when they do, they make better leaders, better teammates, and better contributors to the organization at all levels.

An excellent tool is the Kolbe A™ Index that was developed by the Kolbe Corp in Phoenix, Arizona. Unlike other tests that measure cognition (how you think), or affective behavior (how you feel), the Kolbe A Index measures how you naturally solve problems, get things done, and how you can use your personal innate talents to be most effective. Equally important, it can help you avoid jobs and roles that just might sap your energy, or frustrate you or those around you.

Kathy Kolbe was the first to identify four universal human instincts used in creative problem solving. These instincts are not measurable. However, the observable acts derived from them can be identified and quantified by the Kolbe A Index. These instinct-driven behaviors are represented in the four Kolbe Action Modes:

**Fact Finder** - the instinctive way we gather and share information.

**Follow Thru** - the instinctive way we arrange and design.

**Quick Start** - the instinctive way we deal with risk and uncertainty.

**Implementor** - the instinctive way we handle space and tangibles.

*Note: Kolbe®, the Kolbe A™ Index and the Four Action Modes®
are trademarks of Kathy Kolbe and are used with permission.*

*For more information on individual and team assessments, visit
www.Amilya.com/kolbe
Or go to www.amilya.com/kolbeAindex to take an index and
start learning more about your innate talents today.*

## Keeper's Keys:

**Myth:** In a business context, only business information matters.

**Truth:** In business or in life, the better you understand yourself, the more productive you will be.

**Myth:** If you have the right training and skills, you are the right person for the job.

**Truth:** Not always. As we saw in the story, training and skills can only take you so far. While we each can do a job that is contrary to our conative strengths (how we naturally do things) for a while, it saps our energy and ultimately can negatively affect not only our performance, but how we feel about ourselves.

**Myth:** The grass is always greener on the other side of the fence.

**Truth:** Until you truly understand the value of what is with you and in you on your own side of the fence, you will not be ready to travel to the other side of the fence to discover what is waiting there and make the most of it.

## Food for Thought:

1.  Do you consider yourself – self aware?

2.  How do people describe you?  In your own mind, does that description always fit?

3. How does what you do best and care about the most fit in with what you do today or want to do in the future?

4. If you could design your 'perfect' job or role in your organization, what would it be and what would it look like?

*The Recipe: A Fable for Leaders and Teams*

# <u>ANALYSIS, STRUCTURE AND CONTROL</u>

If change is a constant challenge to us as individuals and as business and team leaders, then analysis, structure and control are the solutions. Right?

They can be, if you strike the right balance. The challenge is to find it.

All businesses need some level of analysis, structure and control. Otherwise, things would fall into chaos. However, too much analysis, structure and control can have the opposite effect, stifling innovation, slowing forward movement and even hampering growth.

Plus, as we saw illustrated in the story about Nate too much oversight and control can damage the cohesiveness and effectiveness of the team. In too many organizations today, BIG Brother is alive and well.

When striking the right balance, you need to ask some important questions.

- Why am I measuring something and what result and I looking for.
- What measurements are the key success indicators for my business or team?
- What process improvements will have the biggest impact on our reaching our goals?
- When is enough, enough?

## Keeper's Keys:

**Myth:** What you don't know can't hurt you.
**Truth:** Details, data and analysis are critical factors in the development, growth, and sustainability of every business. The trick is to find the right balance between flexibility and control.


**Myth:** Once you gain control, it's yours to keep.
**Truth:** Control is fleeting. As difficult as it is to gain control, as soon as you get a handle on it, something may change. It's often just as hard to maintain control as it is to create it.


**Myth:** You know when you in control and when you are not.
**Truth:** We'd like to think so. It's hard to ever truly have 100% control over anything since human behavior and outside factors often can come into play when we least expect it.

**Food for Thought:**

1. Do you like to be in control or do you prefer to delegate control to others? Think of at least two examples.

2. There is a big difference between delegating responsibly and abdicating responsibility. Can you think of examples in your life of either on or both?

3. How do you draw the line between the need for data and analysis paralysis?

4. What is the right balance of control and flexibility for your organization or team?

# <u>MAKING DECISIONS</u>

Leaders are responsible for decisions. What kind of decision maker are you?

As we saw in the story, different types of leaders reach decisions in very different ways. For Allan, Ivan, and Oliver, the action of independent decision making is natural. Leaders like Yale and Sam need a collaborative process with the opportunity to study the facts and get input from others while leaders like Nate look for answers within structured and controlled systems.

There is no right or wrong in the decision making style, but often a blended approach is best. At times, too much independence can lead to tunnel vision or costly mistakes. If we do not seek outside input, we run the risk of overlooking key factors that will affect the results of our decisions. Equally, if our decision making process grinds to a halt while we continually seek more and more data or get bogged down in red tape, we can miss great opportunities or critical deadlines.

The beauty of surrounding yourself with a great team is that when you do, you have a range of talents and experiences to draw from, as well as insights into the resources you may need.

But never forget, at the end of the allotted time you need to ensure that whether it is the team, or the leader, making the decision, that a decision does get made and that you move forward together.

**Keeper's Keys:**


**Myth:** There is only one right way to make decisions.
**Truth:** There is no right or wrong decision making style, but in many cases a blended or situational approach will serve you best.


**Myth:** You need to know you are right before moving forward on a decision.
**Truth:** It would be so much easier if that was the way things always work. But rarely do we have complete information when making decisions. Dealing with uncertainty is part of the decision making process.

**Myth:** Most leaders have one personal decision making style.
**Truth:** For most of us, the best decision making style is going to be situational. When the decision is not that critical (e.g., what's for lunch), any style will do. But when it matters most, consciously choosing HOW the decision will be made can be have a big impact on the final outcome.

*The Recipe: A Fable for Leaders and Teams*

## Food for Thought:

1. When you have a BIG decision to make, what is your natural decision making style?

2. Can you think of a time when consciously choosing not to decide was the right strategy?

3. Who is on your personal team, at home or at work, that you go to most often if you need help with a decision? Why is this person your choice?

4. What are some of the TOOLs that you use to help you make decisions? (Hint: see the list of Utensils on page 118.)

# COMMUNICATION

Communication is the glue or paste that forms a bond between leaders and teams, and that holds great teams together.

We communicate through our words to engage, to inform, to direct, to inspire, and to motivate. But more often than not, it is our actions that serve as the true evidence of the message we ultimately deliver.

Sam has the gift for sharing ideas and holding the attention of his audience, just as his brother Oliver motivates others with his excitement and energy.

We've all met or heard great speakers. They may be clergy, or politicians or the president of the PTA. But to these individuals, works are a way of bringing people together and moving them forward.

But the best communicators over time have paired the talent of speaking and writing with an even greater gift, the ability to listen. When you listen, you have the opportunity to garner information, build on the ideas of others, and to then adapt your words so that communication is more effective. As a listener, you have the ability then to reach out, and show that the speaker is heard, creating a sense of validation and meaning to both your message and theirs. When you don't listen, you soon find that others may stop listening to you.

The last key point in communication is believability. Do your listeners believe that you can do what you say? The best way to ensure that they do is to keep your promises. Words will only take a leader or a team so far. In the end it will always be actions that communicate the strongest message.

## Keeper's Keys:

**Myth:** Communication is always delivered in words.
**Truth:** More often than not, what you do and how you do it will have a much greater impact than just what you say.

**Myth:** You can be a great communicator without being a great listener.
**Truth:** You can be an awesome speaker without listening. But you won't be a great communicator.

**Myth:** Listening is enough.
**Truth:** In life, as in business, listening is important but equally so it that your word and actions reflect that you not only listen, but that you hear and understand

**Myth:** It is a leaders' right to speak for others.
**Truth:** It is a leaders' privilege to speak for others. To earn the privilege you need to listen to others, so that what you say "I speak for all of you."

## Food for Thought:

1.  If you do not know what your message is and the results you hope to get when you deliver it, your communications fall short.  Use this space to refine your message

2.  What are the tools you use to deliver your message? Do you use them as well as you could?

3. Recall one of the best communicators you have ever met. What made them special?

4. How can you work with your team to promote better communication?

# BUILDING CHAMPIONSHIP TEAMS

If it were easy to build championship teams, every team would be a champion.

Great teams are not just found on the playing field. They are in our homes, our schools, our businesses, and our communities.

Winning teams have the right players, the right attitude and a good coach. Championship teams have that something extra – heart. Together, they demonstrate solid leadership through their values and their commitment to reaching the goal

There is cohesiveness and a sense of responsibility to the goal, and to each of our teammates, that makes championship teams unique. They may be made up of superstars but most often they are not. Either way, together they are a force to be reckoned with.

Championship teams know how to play off each other. Multiple players with different talents come together in a way that is supportive and productive. Because of this, they reach the goal over and over again.

A championship team's attitude is focused on the team and the team's mission, not the individual champions. They lose together, learn together, and go on to win together. It is not about a single star player, personality or talent.

Championship teams, on the home front, in business, or in the community have one thing in common, their focus on shared values and a commitment to reaching their goals.

Great teams have great coaches. The role of the coach is to bring out the best in each player just as Mary coached her Givvantake team to their own personal and professional victory. Sometimes a coach is a friend or a parent, sometimes a mentor, but is always honest. The coach's job is not to make you feel good all the time but rather to help you along the journey so that in the end, together with your team, you can say proudly – we accomplished this together.

Sometimes the leader is also the coach, at other times an individual leader is needed, or multiple leaders within the team depending on the situation. But one thing is for sure. Championship teams have a shared commitment to the team's values and goals. They respect each other and the unique talents that each of them brings to the equation.

*The Recipe: A Fable for Leaders and Teams*

They know their individual strengths and how to depend on others to supplement the areas where they may not be as strong. For this reason, they are always on the lookout for a new player who can bring to the team the talents they may lack or need.

Otherwise, no matter how great the individual players may be, you'll never assemble a championship team.

## Keeper's Keys:

**Myth:** Championship teams need a superstar to make them a champion.
**Truth:** In many cases a superstar can be more of a liability than an asset in building a championship team.

**Myth:** The person who scores the most is the natural leader.
**Truth:** Not necessarily. Not all great individual contributors make great leaders. And many of them will be the first to tell you that. A skill that may make someone great at crossing the finish or goal line may not be the same skill that is needed to bring a team together and lead them to victory.

**Myth:** Coaches win games.
**Truth:** Coaches don't win games. Some have never even played them. But a great coach gives the individual players and the team the support, direction and guidance so that they can win.

**Myth:** The leader is always THE leader.
**Truth:** True leaders demonstrate leadership, no matter what their role is in the organization. Positions and titles do not define leaders, actions do.

## Food for Thought:

1. How do you define a "Champion"?

2. What would you describe as the top three talents you bring to your team?

3. What are the top three things you look for in a teammate?

4. How are a coach and a leader different?

# RECOGNITION AND REWARDS

Who does not want to be recognized at some level for a job well done?

Recognition and rewards drive human behavior. And, human behavior drives results. Recognition validates people, their purpose, and their life.

That does not mean that everyone measures and values recognition and rewards in the same way.

In tangible forms, recognition and reward can be as simple as a thank you, recognition for effort or results in a meeting with peers or superiors, or a simple pat on the back.

In other cases, recognition and reward take on a more tangible form as positions of authority, special benefits, or cold hard cash.

Many studies have shown that intangible rewards can have an even greater impact on employee satisfaction and motivation than tangible ones such as title and pay levels.

Recognition and reward are usually tied to performance. Therefore, to increase performance, increase the effectiveness <u>and relevance</u> of your recognition and rewards systems.

## Keeper's Keys:

**Myth**: Desiring recognition or a reward makes you selfish.
**Truth:** Seeking recognition, approval, or reward is a natural behavior, not a selfish one. For some, the reward of personally knowing that you did well is enough. Others may need more outward or tangible examples for it to be meaningful.

**Myth**: All rewards motivate all people equally.
**Truth:** Different people have different values. Recognition and rewards must be relevant to both the giver and the receiver to be truly effective.

**Myth:** Only big rewards matter.
**Truth:** When it's deserved, recognition and reward can have a big impact, but they do not always have to be tied to a big thing. Sometimes some personal recognition or a simple thank you can have even more impact than an annual pay raise, especially if everyone got the same percentage, no matter what their level of effort or achievements were.

## Food for Thought:

1.  What were some examples of intangible rewards that were demonstrated in *The Recipe*?

2.  Can you recall a time when you received an unexpected recognition or reward? What impact did it have on you? How did it affect those around you?

3. Can you recall a time when you felt overlooked for recognition or reward that you believed you deserved? How did that impact you?

4. How comfortable are you with giving recognition and rewards to others?

# CREATING LEARNING EXPERIENCES

We all learn differently, but learn we must. Another key role of leaders is to create learning experiences for their teams so that individually and together they can achieve their goals.

We all have a desire to learn and grow. It may be personally or professionally, but when we stop learning we stop growing. If you want your team to engage – give them an opportunity to learn.

It is commonly accepted theory that there are three primary learning styles:

**Visual** – processing lessons through what they read, what they can see, and what they can visualize.

**Auditory** – processing lessons through what they hear, stories they hear, and verbally repeating the lessons they have learned.

**Kinesthetic Learners** – learn hands on by doing, feeling or touching.

Thus as leaders of teams we need to understand that our teammates may need to have information shared and lessons delivered in a variety of ways.

If you and your team take advantage of the insights that can be gained from the Kolbe A™ Index that can be found on www.Amilya.com/Kolbe or www.Amilya.com/KolbeAIndex, you will find great examples of how information can be delivered to address the needs of different learning styles with a combination of written feedback, auditor sections where Kathy Kolbe explains your special and unique talents via audio playback.

But for many of us, the best way we learn is simply by experiencing and then sharing the experience with others. As you read in *The Recipe,* Mary led the team by helping them discover the lessons they would need along the journey. She did not tell them what they needed to know outright, but rather set up a series of experiences so that they could reach their own destinations and answers.

You, too, can do this for your teams. Like Mary, you want to set up a safe environment where team members can learn and experiment, with you standing by as the leader or coach to guide them. It is the lessons of our experience that are the lessons that stay with us the longest, and the ones that make the greatest impact.

For more information regarding learning experiences you can use to compliment your or your team's experience with *The Recipe*, visit www.Amilya.com/TheRecipeInteractive.

Keeper's Keys:

**Myth:** If I tell you once – I have taught you.
**Truth:** People learn in different ways and at different speeds. Simply issuing an instruction or telling someone how to do something does not ensure that a lesson has been learned.

**Myth:** Leadership can be learned from a book.
**Truth:** Leadership lessons might be found in a book like this one, but to actually learn leadership, you must practice it –daily.

**Myth:** It's like riding a bike – once you know how to do it, you've got it for life.
**Truth:** You may still know how to ride that bike but if you haven't done so in a long time, you are less likely to try. And when you do, you might just find that it is not as easy as you remember. Well developed skills in life or business require continual use to be the best.

## Food for Thought:

1. As a leader, what are the lessons you still have to learn?

2. What kind of a learner are you?  What do you need to reinforce your learning experience?  (Hint:  see page 174)

3.  What are the lessons you want to help your team to learn?

4.  How do the lessons we learn at home carry over to the work place or visa versa?

# About The Author:

Amilya Antonetti spent the first years of her son's life in hospital emergency rooms.

That battle to save her son's life led to not only a wondrous solution but also to the launch of Amilya's Soapworks. A decade later, not only had she moved her natural products into the major grocery chains across the USA and Canada, she helped to redefine the cleaning aisle and usher in the "human and earth friendly" movement which consumers are embracing in waves today.

A popular personality on television and radio, Amilya has appeared on The Oprah Winfrey Show, as a regular guest on The BIG Idea with Donny Deutsch, FOX Strategy Room, CBS This Morning, Extra, and countless international radio and television shows.

Her story of Amilya's Soapworks has appeared in books, newspapers, magazines such as *Chicken Soup for the Entrepreneurial Soul, People, Working Mother, First for Woman, Smart Money, Inc., Time*, and her "Smart Choice Mom" lifestyle and organization tips can be read in *Parent and Child* and *Family Circle* Magazines.

Amilya has received numerous entrepreneurial awards and been lauded by her peers. Her first book, *Why David Hated Tuesdays,* has continued to make her a much sought after guest and public speaker. Amilya has addressed audiences alongside the greatest speakers of our generation, including Tony Robbins, Zig Zigler, Oliver North, Katie Couric and Hillary Clinton.

With the sale of Soapworks, she has moved on to the helm of AMA Enterprises and, through Amilya.com, delivers real world information, products and services to help 21st century consumers make smarter, healthier lifestyle choices.

Amilya is living her life doing what she loves: speaking, writing and illuminating the pathway for others. But as busy as she is Amilya never forgets her most important job, which is to be a great mother to her son David and her young daughter. They remain, and will always be, her purpose in life as well as key passion.

---

Website: www.Amilya.com
Twitter: @Amilya
Facebook: Facebook.com/Amilya
LinkedIn: *www.linkedin.com/in/amilya*

---

# Other Books
## by Amilya Antonetti –

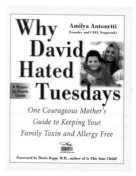

**Why David Hated Tuesdays**

Amilya Antonetti
Founder and CEO, Soapworks

A Room-by-Room Guide

*One Courageous Mother's Guide to Keeping Your Family Toxin and Allergy Free*

Foreword by Doris Rapp, M.D., author of *Is This Your Child?*

A mother's fight to save her son's life and give consumers more choice, ranging from good to better to best.

Amilya Antonetti

with Katherine E. Sansone

Published by Prima Publishing. Roseville, California. Member of the Crown Publishing Group, a division of Random House, Inc.

Available at major bookstores, Amazon.com, and www.Amilya.com

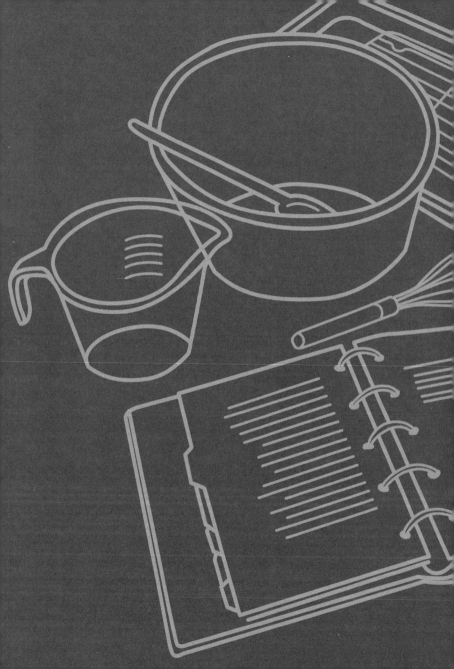